CAMBRIDGE LIBRARY COLLECTION

Books of enduring scholarly value

Literary Studies

This series provides a high-quality selection of early printings of literary works, textual editions, anthologies and literary criticism which are of lasting scholarly interest. Ranging from Old English to Shakespeare to early twentieth-century work from around the world, these books offer a valuable resource for scholars in reception history, textual editing, and literary studies.

Memoir of Mrs Barbauld

Anna Letitia Barbauld (1743–1825), poet, educator and essayist, is now considered to be one of the most important writers of the early Romantic period. Included in her highly regarded works on literary, political, social, and other intellectual topics is the ambitious poem *Eighteen Hundred and Eleven* (1812), which condemned Britain's participation in the Napoleonic Wars. She gained recognition for her influential elementary textbooks *Lessons for Children* (1778–9) and *Hymns in Prose for Children* (1781), which made her name synonymous with the instruction of infants. Her reputation suffered, however, from attacks by critics of her poetry and politics. This charming biography by Anna Letitia Le Breton (1808–85), her great-niece, was first published in 1874 and seeks to bring Barbauld's name back to public attention and acclaim. It draws on personal recollections, letters, and other family memorabilia in the author's possession.

T0370879

Memoir of
Mrs Barbauld

Including Letters and Notices
of her Family and Friends

ANNA LETITIA LE BRETON

CAMBRIDGE
UNIVERSITY PRESS

CAMBRIDGE UNIVERSITY PRESS

Cambridge, New York, Melbourne, Madrid, Cape Town,
Singapore, São Paolo, Delhi, Mexico City

Published in the United States of America by Cambridge University Press, New York

www.cambridge.org
Information on this title: www.cambridge.org/9781108059565

© in this compilation Cambridge University Press 2013

This edition first published 1874
This digitally printed version 2013

ISBN 978-1-108-05956-5 Paperback

From a Medallion by Wedgwood

MEMOIR

OF

MRS. BARBAULD,

INCLUDING

LETTERS AND NOTICES

OF HER FAMILY AND FRIENDS.

BY HER GREAT NIECE

ANNA LETITIA LE BRETON.

LONDON:

GEORGE BELL AND SONS,

YORK STREET, COVENT GARDEN.

1874.

PREFACE.

The writer of the following Memoir is one of the few surviving members of Mrs. Barbauld's family who retains a personal recollection of her, having spent much of her early life under her care, owing her likewise a large debt of gratitude and love. Earnestly desiring to revive some memory of one who though enjoying in her lifetime a considerable amount of literary fame, is now, from the circumstance of her works having been long out of print and difficult to procure, comparatively unknown to the present generation, the author has availed herself of a collection of letters and family papers in her possession, to compile a fuller account of the life and family of Mrs. Barbauld, than her niece Lucy Aikin thought herself justified in doing, when she wrote the original Life, prefixed to the edition of the Works of Mrs. Barbauld, published soon after her death in 1825.

Feelings of delicacy towards members of Mr. Barbauld's family, then living, prevented the true account being given of the unfortunate state of mind with which her husband became afflicted, a calamity which in a great degree crippled her powers for many of the

best years of her life. Many names were also suppress-
ed for reasons no longer existing.

The account of Mrs. Barbauld's ancestors, written
in late years by Miss Aikin, for the benefit of the
younger members of her family; though not intended
for publication, is now printed to shew the influences
which in part formed Mrs. Barbauld's pure and noble
character.

The poems alluded to in the course of the Memoir,
will be found at the end of the volume; as well as her
Essay "On Inconsistency in our Expectations," which
has always been considered one of the most finished of
her prose writings, and was a few years ago printed and
circulated by an unknown friend. The portrait prefixed, is from a cameo, for which she sat about the
year 1773, at the request of her valued friend Josiah
Wedgwood.

Hampstead, 1874.

CONTENTS.

————◆————

MEMOIR.

MEMOIR.

ANNA LETITIA, the eldest child, and only daughter of John Aikin, D.D. and Jane his wife, daughter of the Rev. John Jennings, was born at the village of Kibworth Harcourt in Leicestershire, on the 20th June, 1743.

The following particulars relating to her family, are taken from some unpublished memorials written by the late Lucy Aikin, her niece.

"John Aikin, my great grandfather," says Miss Aikin, "transferred himself at an early age from the Scotch town of Kircudbright to London. How long this place

B

had been the *seat of the Aikins,* or what
station they held there, I cannot say, all
that my father knew on the subject was,
that the family arms were registered in the
Herald's Office at Edinburgh ; consequently
that they, like Scotchmen in general, laid
claim to ' Gentle blood,' however little they
might possess of the world's wealth.

Of the career of my great grandfather in
London, I am equally uninformed, till he
became the master of a linen draper's shop
in that part of Newgate Street than called
Blowbladder Street, from the vicinity of the
great meat market of the city. He appears
at this time to have been a man of substance,
and he took to wife Anne Bentall, whose
father was deacon of the congregation of that
Daniel Burgess of whom Swift has left us an
amusing notice in the Tatler, showing him
to be more rogue than fool in his fanatical
rants. An old portrait of my great grandmother which I have seen, represented her
with nothing striking about her except a
profusion of long ringlets, which had certainly nothing of Puritan primness. My

father had a great notion that she was a
very silly woman, and handed down to his
posterity this one anecdote of her. Some
few months before the birth of her eldest
son, walking with her husband in the fields,
she was siezed with a violent longing to crop
a few mouthfuls of the tempting herbage.
In those days, as we have all heard, any
fancy of a matron under such circumstances
must be gratified at all events. Precious
privilege, now lost to the sex! Down therefore went the dame on hands and knees and
grazed. To this circumstance my father
added, that his father, between jest and
earnest, would ascribe his rural tastes!

This couple had three sons, of whom my
grandfather was the eldest. He was at
first destined for commerce, and placed in
a mercantile house as *French clerk*. I presume he had acquired this language at his
school, the master of which was probably
no deep classic, but having been an actor,
taught him that impressive declamation of
English verse for which he was always distinguished. An ardent love of study, and

conscious power of intellect, soon rendered
the routine of the counting house insupport-
able to him, and he prevailed upon an indulgent father to enter him a pupil of the
Kibworth Academy, afterwards removed to
Northampton.

Of this institution, by the early death
of my great grandfather, the Rev. John
Jennings, Dr. Doddridge had become the
head, but so recently that young Aikin was
his first pupil............The prosperity of my
great grandfather gradually forsook him.
What I have been told was merely this;
that not being so sharp as his countrymen,
he allowed them to make a prey of him. In
the end he gave up business, and found an
asylum with his worthy son at Kibworth.
A long old age it was; he survived to the age
of 92.

My great-great grandfather Jennings was
a clergyman, in what was then called Pow-
island, and a part of Wales; and was one
of the noble 2000 who resigned their livings
rather than violate conscience at the promp-
ting of that treacherous bigot Lord Claren-

don. The loss was the heavier to Mr. Jennings from his cure being his own advowson. I know not what carried him to Kibworth, so remote from his native country, for he was a Welshman—but I believe he was the founder of the Academy afterwards carried on by his son. This son, the Rev. John Jennings, was a very industrious teacher, and a man of letters............After the passing of the Toleration Act, he became the dissenting minister of Kibworth. His first wife was a beautiful young girl, only child of one of the principal members of his congregation. Seven months after marriage she produced a babe, small and puny, which died almost immediately. Puritan rigor was little disposed in such a case, to grant to a suspected offender the benefit of even the most reasonable doubt. An old hag of the congregation, gained or forced admittance to the bedside of the new mother, to tell her, weak and exhausted as she was, the evil thoughts of *all the world* on this occasion. The poor young creature wept

all the rest of the day, and died the next.
When the widower married a second time,
the father of her who had been 'done to
death by slanderous tongues,' said to him,
'call your first daughter Jane, after my
poor girl, and I will give her a *rood land.*'
How much this means I know not, but his
daughter, my grandmother, was named
Jane, and had the land. Her husband sold
it when they removed from Kibworth to
Warrington.

My great grandmother, the second wife of
Mr. Jennings, was Anna Letitia, one of the
many daughters of Sir Francis Wingate of
Harlington Grange, Beds., by the Lady
Anne, daughter of Sir Arthur Annesley,
first Earl of Anglesey, and Lord Privy Seal
under Charles II. Her name of Anna, I
suppose she bore in compliment to her
mother; Letitia, was an appellation brought
into the Wingate family long before. Lettice
Wingate, a nun, is commemorated in the
pedigree book at Harlington, as having
taught her nephew to read.

The old family house,* on the most an-
tique end of which, my uncle remembered a
plate bearing the date 1396, was the seat of
a family, Norman I presume, of the name
of Belverge; bearing on their shield three
pears *or* (bel verger) till it was conveyed by
the marriage of an heiress at the end of the
14th century, to a Wingate of the neighbouring village of Sharpenhoe. Wingate of
Harlington, is included in the list of gentry
made by the Heralds' College on their visi-
tation, held in the reign, and under the
auspices of Henry VI; which intimates
him to have belonged to the Lancastrian
party. The master of the Grange was never
Lord of the Manor, therefore only the
second *great man* of Harlington; yet his
estates appear to have been considerable.
Edward Wingate held the exalted office of

---

* The house still stands; at present occupied by
George Pearse, Esq., who married Elizabeth, the only
child of Mrs. Aikin's brother, John Wingate Jennings,
the last of the name. This lady, who never quitted her
old home, died a few years ago at a ripe age in the house
in which she was born, beloved and respected by all
who knew her.

' Master of the Bears,' to Queen Elizabeth.
Sir Francis, in his elaborate letter of declara-
tion to the Lady Anne, still preserved, I
think, values his estate at 1000 per annum,
and promises to keep a coach and six. The
Earl, her father, gave her several thousand
pounds. Bishop Burnet writes of this noble
lord, that he had sold himself so often that
at length no party thought him worth buy-
ing. He seems indeed to have feathered
his nest pretty well, but was certainly an
able man. We may take comfort, roguery
is not hereditary, folly often is.

Grand were the preparations made at
poor Harlington for the reception of the
bride. The hall and *state bedchamber* over
it, were fitted up on the occasion. The
chamber was hung with tapestry, 'disfigur-
ing and representing' the judgment of
Paris, and other classical stories ; the bed
was of crimson damask, richly adorned with
fringe and gilding ; there was a handsome
Japan cabinet, heavy arm chairs, and toilet
ornaments to match, and a dressing room

within; splendors which excited my youthful awe and veneration, decayed and faded as they were,—but as for Lady Anne, tradition says that she sat her down and cried when she saw to how poor a place she had been brought as her future home. Her husband looks in his portrait very good natured, but heavy enough—the Lady Anne—let us hope she was of a sweeter temper than she looks in her's. She was a stiff presbyterian, her husband a jolly episcopalian, who said somewhat bitterly, that when he was gone she would certainly turn his great hall into a conventicle. Perhaps this thought had set an edge on his zeal, when, in the character of a Justice of the Quorum, he committed John Bunyan to Bedford gaol for unlicensed preaching. The only memorable action of his life, as far as I am aware.

But that an old family mansion must absolutely have a ghost, in fact it would be almost as disgraceful to the race to be without one as to want a coat without arms, I would not be so undutiful to my great-great grandmother as to tell the tale, but it is a

matter of necessity, so here it is. The lady
Anne had a friend who unknown to her
husband had made up a purse, the contents
of which she destined to be shared among
her children by a former marriage. On her
deathbed she entrusted to her this deposit.
Lady Anne, I dare not say ,with what
thoughts, she being then a widow, and hard
pressed enough, *delayed* to deliver over the
money. One night, she was startled by a
mysterious rustling in a certain long, dark,
crooked passage into which her chamber
opened ; the rustling—yes, she could not
be mistaken—of a silk gown, the very gown
of her departed friend. It passed on to a
certain narrow door, at which *something*
seemed to enter, and the rustling ceased.
Her ladyship paid the money next day, and
nothing was ever heard or seen more ; but
some people had an odd feeling as they
passed that door, leading only to the china
closet, within my memory.

A more favorable trait of Lady Anne has
been preserved. She possessed two beautiful miniatures, evidently a pair ; one

represented her brother, Lord Altham, the
other a lady, so lovely in feature, and still
more in expression, one was never weary of
gazing upon it. Lady Anne was accustom-
ed often to take it out of her cabinet and
weep tenderly over it; so far her daughters
could attest from their own knowledge, but
she would never inform them whom it
represented, or what had been her story.
Lord Altham, worthy to shine amongst the
courtiers of Charles II, had three wives
living at the same time; the first of these
deceived and unhappy ladies was probably
his sister's friend; yes, it must have been
her wrongs over which she shed these frequent tears; and shame at her brother's
treachery and wickedness doubtless tied her
tongue.

Sir Francis died in middle age, leaving
his lady with three sons, and six ill por-
tioned daughters. Some few notices have
reached me of all the six sisters. Mr.
Moore, the husband of the eldest, was a
clergyman, very poor, very honest, and the
simplest of the simple. He would some-

times borrow a trifle of his mother-in-law,
giving her an acknowledgment in these
cautious terms, 'I promise to pay, if I am
able.' 'My dear' he once cried out to his
wife, 'a great rude girl came and robbed our
apple tree while I was in the garden.' 'And
did you let her?' 'How could I help it?'
Neither could he help his sons going to
ruin. Another sister married a Dr. Hay,
a Scotch physician. She was accounted a
wit, and one or two of her *good things* I have
heard, but should be sorry to recite in the
' ears polite ' of a younger generation.

The sons all possessed the estate in succession. The first dissipated more than his
prudent brother was able to retrieve. The
third, John, a retired naval captain, just
managed to make both ends meet. He was
long a widower, and as he had no surviving
child, it was a matter of anxious speculation
which nephew he would make his heir.
Charles Moore, eldest nephew, chose to regard it as his right, and prepared himself
for the enjoyment of the few ancestral acres
by such a course of idleness, extravagance,

and folly, as determined his uncle never to put them at his mercy. For the opposite qualities he at length declared it to be his intention to leave the old place to my grandfather, Arthur Jennings.

By way of retaliation I suppose, for his persecution of Bunyan, two of the daughters of Sir Francis married dissenting ministers, not in his lifetime, however. One was Mrs. Norris, the other was Anna Letitia, my great grandmother. One died single, aunt Rachel, of whom all I know is that she had the honor to have Rachel, lady Russell, for her Godmother; the families being in some way related.*

---

* She was niece to Lady Anglesey, and the Wingates seem to have taken advantage of the relationship to push their fortune, though without success, by the following passage in Lady Russell's Letters.

"We are told that Mr. Middleton is in a dying condition,—his place in the Prize Office is worth about 400 a year. My cousin lady Anne Wingate would be contented if it could be obtained for Sir Francis. Lord Bedford and myself would show our readiness to serve my Lady Anne and Sir Francis, and the more friends joyn will not recommend it less to my Lord Devonshire, if he can do anything in it. I have writ to him Lord Bedford's thoughts of Sir Francis; which are, that he is an understanding, honest, gentleman, and has almost

My great grandmother was left a rather young and slenderly provided widow, with four children, Arthur, John, Francis, and Jane, my grandmother Aikin. She continued to reside at Kibworth : Dr. Doddridge, her husband's successor as head of the academy, was boarded in her house. Her children were indebted to him for much early instruction, which contributed with their advantages of birth and connections to raise them in the estimation of their neighbours above the level of a narrow fortune. My grandmother was presented at court by a lady of the Annesley connection, no small distinction in those days. She was sprightly, not without personal charms, and had a natural talent for singing. The result of the whole was, that her honored tutor was moved to indite an elaborate epistle, still preserved, in which he labored to convince her, that it was actually possible

---

exceeded any in this country in his zeal and activeness towards the present Government."
To Lord Devonshire, 1690.

* Dr. Doddridge's letter is in the appendix.

for a grave divine of thirty years of age to experience the passion of love for a little gentlewoman of fifteen. The converse of the problem he seems to have taken for granted ; not so the young lady, who stedfastly refused to become the Eloise of such an Abelard. Arthur her eldest brother, was my grandfather, my elder brothers could a little remember him, but he died before my birth. I have often regretted it; all I ever heard of him was delightful. My father used to say he had as much of the milk of human kindness as ever man had, and had a rich vein of humor, and told a story admirably. He was short, broad-chested, and of extraordinary strength. His span was eleven inches, and he would say he feared no man if he could once get him within his *grip*. He would walk when a gay young man from London to Harlington,* six or

---

* The village of Harlington is very near the great chalk downs of Dunstable, at this time one of the hunting grounds of the famed Dick Turpin and his gang. One morning Mr. Jennings own horse was found in the stable, heated, trembling, and covered with foam ; evidently having been ridden all night. Another time Mrs. Jennings was going to town for the winter, and travelling

eight and thirty miles to a dance, and walk
back next morning. He had the bright
hazel eye of the Wingates.

His brother John, destined for a dissenting minister was the wit of Dr. Doddridge's
academy, and the darling of his relations
and friends. A diary of Mr. Merivale his
fellow-student records several of the smart
sayings and merry stories of 'Jack.' Soon
after he had finished his education, he went
to live in a kind of chaplain capacity with
Mr. Coward, a wealthy merchant I believe,
who left the fund which still bears his name,
for the education of dissenting teachers. A
chaplain, this zealous puritan appears not
greatly to have needed, since he took upon
himself the performance of the family de-
votions. On these occasions he would be

---

over the downs towards evening (she always slept on the
road) they perceived a horseman persistently keeping
pace with them. This went on some time, till Mrs.
Jennings got into such a state of alarm and nervousness
that she could bear it no longer, and putting her head
out of the carriage window, she called out, "If you want
to rob us, *do!*" "Lord bless me madam," cried a familiar
voice, "rob you! I am only John so and so, keeping up
with the carriage for company."

carried out in prayer to very extraordinary lengths indeed, according to the reports of Uncle Jack, faithfully preserved by his contemporaries. He had once insured for a considerable sum a ship called the Mingen, which was lost. Accounting himself ill-treated by the Deity on the occasion, he thus remonstrated—'But O Lord! thou *nickedst* me in the Mingen.'

Let us now return to my grandfather Aikin. Among his fellow-students was Mr. Merivale afterwards a dissenting minister at Exeter, whose diary communicated to me by his grandson (the late John Herman Merivale one of the Judges in Bankruptcy,) is curiously illustrative of the simplicity of the age. ' He and Aikin,' he says, ' set out from London for the Academy on the same day. Aikin having two younger brothers to take to school, travelled by the wagon, but I did not choose it, for it would have cost half-a-guinea !' Therefore he walked by the side.

After quitting Doddridge's Academy, my grandfather went to the university of Aberdeen, then I believe illustrated by a school of learned and able theologians, such as Lowman and the Fordyces who were casting off the fetters of Calvin. My grandfather settled at length in what was called low Arianism, which subsequently became, under his tuition, the system of the Warrington divines, almost without exception. That his University regarded him as an alumnus to be proud of, was evinced by its degree of D.D. conferred upon him at Warrington, not alone without solicitation but without notice. In fact to his humble and retiring temper, the distinction was actually distressing, and he would have been well pleased to shut up his diploma in a drawer, and say nothing about it to any one. He had just married and accepted the invitation of a congregation at Market Harborough, when an affection of the chest ascribed to a fall, compelled him to resign his pulpit, and look to tuition as his sole resource. A letter to his friend Merivale explains his circumstances with a charming simplicity. Twelve pounds per annum for board, lodging and the instruction of such a man! But he had his reward in the attachment, the veneration, of his scholars; in the atmosphere of respect and admiration which everywhere surrounded him; and his gains were adequate to his humble wants, his modest wishes. He left behind him as the savings of his life, with some small additions probably on the side of his wife, about five-and twenty hundred pounds.

In my first visit to Liverpool, twenty years after my grandfather's death, I several times met with elderly or middle-aged gentlemen who showed me attentions I was at a loss to account for, till I found they all boasted of having been my grandfather's pupils. Not twenty years since a gentleman introduced himself with 'I was at your grandfather's funeral.'

It was his constant care never, even by inadvertence to do the smallest hurt to any human creature. To this principle he gave a last token of adherence in his positive direction not to be buried within the walls of the Meeting-house, but in the open

Churchyard. After resigning his tutorship, shortly before his death, he calmly said that he had now nothing to do either for this world or another.

A letter from his widow (Dr. Doddridge's Miss Jenny) is touching in its piety and resignation.

To Mrs. Barbauld. Jan. 1st, 1781.

My dear Child,

It is a considerable alleviation of the heavy stroke that is fallen upon me that I have children who were sensible of the worth of their excellent father, and I believe sincerely lament the loss of him, and tenderly sympathise with their afflicted mother, let us mingle our tears and pay that best tribute of honour and love to his memory, the imitating his virtues. I am indeed greatly afflicted, and the few remaining days of my pilgrimage will be sorrowful, oh! may it be that sorrow by which the heart is made better! may His gracious purpose be answered that I may have reason to say, it is good for me that I have been afflicted. Nor

would I ungratefully forget His past boun-
ties, my whole life has been a life of mercies;
my union with your dear father was a
constant source of happiness; very few
couples have lived so long together; peace
and plenty crown'd our days, we saw our
children brought up, saw them virtuous,
esteemed, beloved, and comfortably settled
in the world; and when increasing infir-
mities no longer permitted my dearest
partner to labour in his Lord's vineyard, he
was called to receive his reward, and has
left a name behind him that will reflect an
honor on his latest posterity. On his account we ought to rejoice, his constitution
was so worn that had he continued longer,
his sufferings would probably have been
greater than his enjoyments, let us therefore
say from our hearts, the Lord gave, the Lord
has taken away, blessed be the name of the
Lord.

It would have been a soothing consolation
if your poor father had been able to take
such a last leave of us as his piety and love
would have dictated, but alas! he was so

oppressed with the violence of his distemper, that I believe that though he was sensible he had not the command of his thoughts, and his asthma was so severe that he could scarce collect breath to utter a short sentence. Two or three times he pressed me to go to bed, and whenever I gave him anything said with his usual complaisance, ' thank you my dear,' and when I asked him if he would have Dr. Turner called in, said with some calmness, no, no ; but gave no intimation that he was apprehensive of his approaching change. The few words I have mentioned were (in a manner) all he spoke during his short illness ; t'is a satisfaction to me that I never left him from the time he was seized till I closed those eyes which were the light of my life. Your brother saw him expire, and was affected as a son ought to be ; he and your sister have shewn me every attention and tenderness, and press me to live with them. I have not yet determined how I shall dispose of myself, but if upon mature consideration I have reason to think that it will be neither inconvenient nor disagreeable to them, it seems the most eligible asylum I could chuse. Was I to continue in my present solitary situation, I believe I should sink under it. Pray for your poor mother, that I may attain to a calm submission to the divine will, and so live that I may again meet with the dear partner of my soul in that happy world where all tears shall be wiped away, and there shall be no more death.

I am ever your affectionate Mother,
JANE AIKIN.

Dr. and Mrs. Aikin had two children, Anna Letitia, afterwards Mrs. Barbauld, and her brother John, the writer and physician, four years younger than herself.

That quickness of apprehension by which she was distinguished shewed itself from her earliest infancy. Her mother says in a letter, in which after gently bewailing the backwardness of her grand-children, Edmund and Lucy, both under four, 'I once indeed knew a little girl who was as eager to learn as her instructors could be to teach

her, and who at two years old could read
sentences and little stories in her *wise book*,
roundly, without spelling; and in half a
year more could read as well as most women;
but I never knew such another, and I believe
never shall." The earliest event she used
to speak of as remembering, was the stir in
the family caused by the news of the entrance
of the Pretender's Army into England in
1745, she then being three years old. Kibworth being in the high road to London,
the question of their immediate removal
was anxiously discussed, till the news of the
defeat of the rebels put an end to their
alarms.

To resume Miss Aikin's narrative.—"Her
mother, a woman of sense and a gentlewoman said, that there was no alternative
for a girl brought up in a boy's school,
between being a prude and hoyden. She
preferred the first, rightly, no doubt, if the
case must be so, but it was owing to this
training, I presume, that Mrs. Barbauld
never appeared at her ease, nor felt so, as
she has often told me, in general society.

Ceremonious she was, and humble to strangers to a degree which sometimes provoked one. Strangers would sometimes say they could not be afraid of her, she was so unassuming, which was true. In her youth, great bodily activity, and a lively spirit struggled hard against the tight rein which held her. London cousins wondered sometimes at the gymnastic feats of the country lass. It was these perhaps, added to the brightness of her lilies and roses which sunk so deep into the heart of Mr. Haynes, a rich farmer of Kibworth. He followed this damsel of fifteen to Warrington and obtained a private audience of her father, and begged his consent to make her his wife. My grandfather answered that his daughter was then walking in the garden, and he might go and ask her himself. With what grace the farmer pleaded his cause I know not ; but at length out of all patience at his unwelcome importunities, she ran nimbly up a tree which grew by the garden wall, and let herself down into the lane beyond, leaving her suitor '*planté là.*' The poor man went home disconsolate ; he lived and died a bachelor ; though he was never known to purchase any other book whatever, 'the works of Mrs. Barbauld' splendidly bound adorned his parlour to the end of his days. This whole story I heard from an old servant of the family, and my aunt who was present, did not contradict it in a single word.

My father had a notion that her deportment alarmed young men, and rather struck them 'with amazement and blank awe' than won their hearts, but this was surely a mistake, I know three or four of her lovers who never ceased to regard her with affection as well as admiration. Her conversation in her happiest moods had a charm inexpressible ; wit, playful wit, tempered with true feminine softness, and the gentle dignity of a high mind, unwont to pour forth its hidden treasures on all demands.

She observed to me once, that she had never been placed in a situation which suited her. It was true, unless the bright years of Warrington might be excepted. She had then her father, her brother, the

academic body, and a crowd of admirers.
But the manner of her home savored no
doubt of puritanical rigor. She and her
mother, neat, punctual, strict, though of
cultivated mind and polished manners, were
thoroughly uncongenial.

The removal of her father, Dr. Aikin, to
Warrington as Theological tutor to the
newly founded Academy (or rather college)
there, took place when she was just fifteen.
Her person is thus described at this time.
' She was possessed of great beauty, distinct traces of which she retained to the
latest period of her life. Her person was
slender, her complexion exquisitely fair with
the bloom of perfect health; her features
regular and elegant, and her dark blue eyes
beamed with the light of wit and fancy.'
The Warrington Academy belongs now
so entirely to the past, that a short account
of it seems almost necessary here; and I
am happy to be allowed to make use of
a most interesting and lively sketch read
by Mr. Henry A. Bright of Liverpool to
the Historic Society of Lancashire and

Cheshire—' In the year 1753 the failure
or decay of the several Academies belonging to the English Presbyterian body
caused no inconsiderable anxiety to the
more thoughtful and earnest among the
liberal dissenters. Where could those
ministers be educated in theology unshackled by creed and doctrine ? On none
did these questions press with greater
weight than on John Seddon, the young
minister at Warrington. The idea of found-
ing a new Academy was never dropped until
it had been carried out in action. How he
worked, and wrote, and explained, and
begged ! He is never discouraged, though
his discouragements are innumerable. He
is never down-hearted though his friends
are always suggesting difficulties and pro-
phesying evil............A circular was sent
round signed by Daniel Bayley (of Manchester), John Lees, afterwards Sir Caryll
Worsley, and seven others ; and in June,
1757, the first general meeting was held.
Lord Willoughby of Parham* was appoint-

---

*His nephew who was one of the first pupils at

ed President. Sir H. Hoghton, Messrs. Heywood and Percival, and other Manchester and Liverpool gentlemen subscribed to take houses in Warrington and appoint tutors for the new Academy. 'The tutors will take boarders into their houses at £15 per annum for those who had two months vacation, and £18 for those who had no vacation.' These terms are however exclusive of tea, washing, fire and candles. The tutors were Dr. Taylor of Norwich, author of the Hebrew Concordance, whose learning was so generally acknowledged that all the English and Welch Bishops and Archbishops, with but four exceptions, were subscribers to the work. Mr. Holt was mathematical tutor, and Dr. Aikin languages and literature, and after Dr. Taylor's death, divinity; Dr. Priestley, Dr. Enfield, and the Rev. Gilbert Wakefield were afterwards appointed. 'The tutors in my time,' says Dr. Priestley, 'lived in the most perfect harmony.

Warrington, was afterwards 17th and last Lord Willoughby of Parham; the last also of the old Presbyterian nobility of England.

We drank tea together every Saturday, and our conversation was equally instructive and pleasing,—we were all Arians, and the only subject of much consequence on which we differed respected the doctrine of the Atonement, concerning which Dr. Aikin held some obscure notions.'

In the letter of invitation from Mr. Seddon to Dr. Aikin at Kibworth, one passage is curious, as showing what travelling in England was a hundred years ago. 'Mr. Holland has given us some reason to hope y^t you will come over to Warrington in the Easter week, in order to take a view of y^r future situation; if so, give me leave to recomend ye following plan. I'll suppose you set out from Kibworth on Sunday afternoon; as you intend travelling in post-chaises, you'l easily reach Loughborough, or perhaps Derby that night, ye next night you may come to Offerton, w^h is about a mile short of Stockport, where I am with Mrs. Seddon, and will be ready to receive you and wait upon you to Warrington; you will do well to come prepared for riding, for you will not meet with any carriages at Stockport; nor are the roads to Warrington proper for them; when you get to a place called Bullock's Smithy, about two miles short of Stockport, enquire for Offerton. Mr. Roe, late of Birmingham, now lives there; and we shall be glad to see you. If you'l write to me time enough, and be particular eno^h in your time, I will endeavour to meet you with my own chaise, or send a servant for that purpose.'

Besides the students, distinguished strangers came to Warrington to consult the tutors, or visit the students. Howard the Philanthropist came in order that the younger Aikin might revise his MSS and correct his proofs. Roscoe of Liverpool came, and first learned to care for Botany from his visits to the Warrington Botanical Gardens. Pennant the Naturalist; Currie, the biographer of Burns; and many a Presbyterian minister, eminent then, though now forgotten—were among the visitors to the Athens of our county. But there were other attractions besides the tutors and their philosophy. 'We have a knot of lasses just after your own heart' writes Mrs. Barbauld, then Miss Aikin, to her friend Miss Belsham 'as merry, blithe and gay, as you could wish; and very smart and clever —two of them are the Miss Rigbys. We have a West Indian family too, that I think you would like; a young couple who seem intended for nothing but mirth, frolic, and gaiety.' It was a sad day for Warrington when Miss Lizzy Rigby became Mrs. Bunny, and Miss Sally Rigby was wooed and wedded by Dr. Parry of Bath :—it was sadder still when the lively West Indian had to slip away from his creditors and leave Warrington for ever—saddest of all was it when 'our poetess' herself, after winning the hearts of half the students, some one or two of whom lived sighing and single for her sake--when she too followed the Miss Rigbys' unfortunate example, and was carried off to Palgrave.' From difficulties in the management of this Academy however, and the deaths of Dr. Taylor, Dr. Aikin, and Mr. Seddon, and the want of sufficient discipline,

—the hopes of the Trustees were but partially realized, and the Academy was closed in 1786, after a useful but precarious existence of nine and twenty years. A College at Manchester was established to which the Warrington Trustees transferred their library—It then removed to York, and has now removed to London. It still retains the old Warrington characteristics of a freedom quite unshackled, a fearless daring in the cause of truth, and a clear and penetrating glance into the deepest problems of theology. An extract from a letter from Lucy Aikin to Mr. Bright will close the subject. ' I have often thought with envy of that society. Neither Oxford nor Cambridge could boast of brighter names in literature or science than several of these dissenting tutors—humbly content in an obscure town, and on a scanty pittance, to cultivate in themselves, and communicate to a rising generation, those mental acquirements and moral habits which are their own exceeding great reward. They and theirs lived together like one large family, and in the facility of their intercourse they found large compensation for its deficiency in luxury and splendor—such days are past—whom have we now ' content with science in a humble shed ? '

It was at Warrington in the year 1773 that the 1st vol. of Miss Aikin's Poems was published. They had an immediate success. The reviews praised, letters of congratulation poured in—from old friends,—from entire strangers. Two of these have been preserved, from Dr. Priestley, whose excellent wife was her dearest friend—and from Mrs. Montagu.

Leeds, 13th June 1769.

Dear Miss Aikin,

You will be surprised when I tell you I write this on the behalf of *Pascal Paoli* and the brave *Corsicans*, but it is strictly true. Mr. Turner of Wakefield, who says he reads your poems not with admiration but astonishment, insists upon my writing to you, to request that a copy of your poem called *Corsica* may be sent to

Mr. Boswell, with permission to publish it
for the benefit of those noble islanders. He
is confident that it cannot fail greatly to pro-
mote their interest now that a subscription
is open for them, by raising a generous ardor
in the cause of liberty, and admiration of
their glorious struggles in its defence. Its
being written by a *lady*, he thinks, will be a
circumstance very much in their favour, and
that of the poem; but there is no occasion
for Mr. Boswell to be acquainted with your
name, unless it be your own choice some
time hence. I own I entirely agree with
Mr. Turner in these sentiments, and therefore hope Miss Aikin will not refuse so
reasonable a request, which will at the same
time lay a great obligation on friends in
England, and contribute to the relief of her
own heroes in Corsica. I consider that you
are as much a general as Tyrtæus was, and
your poems (which I am confident are much
better than his ever were) may have as great
an effect as his. They may be the *coup de
grace* to the French troops in that island,
and *Paoli*, who reads English, will cause

it to be printed in every history in that re-
nowned island.

Without any joke, I wish you would comply with this request. In this case you
have only to send a corrected copy to us at
Leeds, or to Mr. Johnson* in London, and
I will take care to introduce it to the notice
of Mr. Boswell by means of Mr. Vaughan
or Mrs. Macaulay, or some other friends of
liberty and Corsica in London. The sooner
this is done the better. Mr. Turner regrets
very much that it was not done some time
ago.

I shall not tell you what I think of your
poems, for more than twenty reasons, one of
which is that I am not able to express it.
We are now all expectation at the opening
of every packet from Warrington.

My piece on Perspective is nearly ready
for the press. Come and see me before it
is quite printed, and I will engage to teach
you the whole art and mystery of it in a few
hours. If you come a month after, I may
know no more about the matter than any

---

* The publisher of St. Paul's Churchyard.

body else. I am about to make a bolder push than ever for the *pillory*, the *King's Bench Prison*, or something worse. Tell Mr. Aikin he may hug himself that I have no connexion with the Academy. On Monday next Mr. Turner and I set out on a visit to the Archdeacon at Richmond.

With all our compliments to all your worthy family,

I am, with the greatest cordiality,
Your friend and admirer,
J. PRIESTLEY.

Hill Street, Feb. 22nd, 1774.

Dear Madam,

If I had not been prevented by indisposition from making my immediate acknowledgments, you would have been assured before this time of my sense of the favour done to me by your polite letter, and the great pleasure I feel in the opening a more intimate correspondence with Miss Aikin. As the world is in general too much disposed, you are certainly obliged to every man who is not jealous, and every woman

E

who is not envious of your talents ; that I
did not withhold the praise that is due to
them gives me some merit with you, but
that you may not over rate the obligation
I will confess that I act from a perfect and
long experience, that it is more to my personal happiness and advantage to indulge
the love and admiration of excellence, than
to cherish a secret envy of it. To this disposition I owe friendships which have been
the happiness and honour of my life. You
must not expect to find in me, the talents
which adorn the friends around me, I shall
not think myself disgraced in your opinion
if you find something in me to love, tho'
nothing to admire. The genuine effect of
polite letters is to inspire candour, a social
spirit, and gentle manners ; to teach a dis-
dain of frivolous amusements, injurious
censoriousness, and foolish animosities. To
partake of these advantages and to live
under the benign empire of the muses, on
the conditions of a naturalized subject, who,
not having any inherent right to a share of
office, credit, or authority, seeks nothing but

the protection of the society is all I aim at.
I am much pleased with the hope you give
me of adding so valuable an ornament to my
circle of Friends as Miss Aikin. I always
wish to find great virtues where there are
great talents, and to love what I admire, so,
to tell you the truth, I made many enquiries
into your character as soon as I was acquainted with your works, and it gave me infinite
pleasure to find the moral character returned
the lustre it received from the mental accomplishments. Your essays have made
me still more intimately acquainted with the
turn of your mind, more sincerely your
friend, and more warmly your admirer. I
dare not repeat, to you, what I have said of
them to others ; what might, to your modest
diffidence, have the appearance of flattery
would set me at a distance from your friendship to which I aspire. I hope whenever
you come to London you will come before
the Spring is far advanced, for I usually
leave London early in May. Bad health,
and a variety of engagements make me a
remiss correspondent, but I shall at any

time be very happy to hear from you, and happier still if you can suggest anything I can do for your service. If any work appears in the Literary World which you would wish to have convey'd to you, favour me at any time with your commands. Your style is so classical, that I imagine that your Father's Study chiefly abounds with old books, if anything new excites your curiosity let me have the pleasure of conveying it to you. With great esteem,

I am Dear Madam,

Your most obedient and

sincere humble Servant,

ELIZ. MONTAGU.

I made my friend Gen. Paoli very happy by presenting him with your Poems. The muses crown virtue when fortune refuses to do it.

After passing through four editions within twelve months, this first volume was followed, ere the end of the year, by another, in which she and her brother joined : the title was ' Miscellaneous Pieces in Prose, by J. and A. L. Aikin.' These likewise met with much notice and admiration, and have been several times reprinted.

Having thus successfully laid the foundation of a literary reputation, she might have gone on to longer and more important works, had not an event, of the greatest consequence in all women's lives, now taken place which subjected her to new influences, new duties, and station in life.

Shortly before this time, there came as a pupil to the Academy a young Frenchman of the name of Rochemont Barbauld, descended from a family of French Protestants. During the persecutions of Louis XIV, his grandfather, then a boy, was carried on board a ship inclosed in a cask and conveyed to England; and on the marriage of one of the daughters of George II to the Elector of Hesse, was appointed his chaplain, and attended her to Cassel.

At this place his son Rochemont was born. On the breaking up of the household of the Electress he returned to England with his father, who destined him for the Church, but somewhat unadvisedly sent him for instruction to the dissenting Warrington Academy; and from the change of opinions formed there, he felt obliged to renounce his expectations from the Church, though by doing so he raised the further obstacle of want of fortune and profession to the objections already felt by Miss Aikin's parents to his union with their daughter.

Lucy Aikin speaks in strong but no doubt appropriate terms of this event; which, consideration towards surviving members of the Barbauld family, prevented her saying when she first wrote the life of her aunt.

"Her attachment to Mr. Barbauld was the illusion of a romantic fancy—not of a tender heart. Had her true affections been early called forth by a more genial home atmosphere, she would never have allowed herself to be caught by crazy demonstrations of amorous rapture, set off with theatrical French manners, or have conceived of such exaggerated passion as a safe foundation on which to raise the sober structure of domestic happiness. My father ascribed that

ill-starred union in great part to the baleful
influence of the ' Nouvelle Heloise,' Mr. B.
impersonating St. Preux. She was inform-
ed by a true friend that he had experienced
one attack of insanity, and was urged to
break off the engagement on that account.
—' Then ' answered she, ' if I were now to
disappoint him, he would certainly go mad.'
To this there could be no reply ; and with
a kind of desperate generosity she rushed
upon her melancholy destiny. It should
however in justice be said, that a more up-
right, benevolent, generous or independent
spirit than Mr. Barbauld's did not exist, as
far as his malady would permit ; his moral
character did honor to her choice, but he
was liable to fits of insane fury, frightful in
a schoolmaster. Her sufferings with such
a husband, who shall estimate ? Children
this pair seemed immediately to have des-
paired of. My brother Charles, born only
one year after their marriage, was bespoken
by them almost directly, they took him
home with them before he was two years
old—she enjoyed in his dutiful affection—

in the charms of his delightful disposition
—his talents and his accomplished mind,
her pride, her pleasure, the best solace of
her lonely age.   Mrs. Barbauld's indolence
was a standing subject of regret and reproach with the admirers of her genius
—but those who blamed her, little knew
the daily and hourly miseries of her home ;
—they could not compute the amount of
hindrances proceeding from her husband's
crazy habits, and the dreadful apprehensions
with which they could not fail to inspire
her.

At length the blow fell—Mr. B's insanity
became manifest, undeniable, and it took the
unfortunate form of a quarrel with his wife.
Well for her that she had the protection of
an opposite neighbour in her brother !   We
were all of us constantly on the watch as
long as she persisted in occupying the same
house with the lunatic.   Her life was in
perpetual danger.   Then shone forth the
nobleness of her spirit.   She had a larger
share than any woman I ever knew of the
great quality of courage—courage both

physical and moral. She was willing to
expose herself to really frightful danger from
the madman's rage, rather than allow him
to be irritated by necessary restraint. When
all was over and this miserable chapter of
her history finally closed, her genius reas-
serted its claims. Her best poems, her
noble, though not appreciated, 1811—all
those evincing a tenderness she had never
before been known to possess,—bear date
from her widowhood."

Unconscious of the future miseries of her life, Mrs. Barbauld shortly after her marriage prepared to accompany her husband to the village of Palgrave in Suffolk, where he had accepted the charge of a dissenting congregation, and opened a boys' school. Before they had determined upon this plan Mrs. Montagu wrote to propose to her to become the Principal of a kind of Ladies' College which she wished to establish, and in these days it is curious to read in Mrs. Barbauld's answer the reasons she gives for declining the offer. "A kind of Academy for ladies" she says, "where they are to be taught in a regular manner the various branches of science, appears to me better calculated to form such characters as the *Précieuses* or *Femmes Savantes* than good wives or agreeable companions. The best way for a woman to acquire knowledge is from conversation with a father or brother, and by such a course of reading as they may recommend, perhaps you may think that having myself stepped out of the bounds of female reserve in becoming an author, it is with an ill grace I offer these sentiments —but my situation has been peculiar, and would be no rule for others. I should likewise object to the age proposed— geography, languages, &c. are best learned from about nine to thirteen. I should have little hopes of cultivating a love of knowledge in a young lady of fifteen who came to me ignorant and uncultivated : it is too late then to begin to learn. The empire of the passions is coming on—those attachments begin to be formed, which influence the happiness of future life—the care of a mother alone can give suitable attention to this important period. The ease and grace of society ; the duties in their own family,—to their friends, the detail of domestic economy—lastly their behaviour to the other half of their species, who then begin to court their notice —these are the accomplishments which a young woman has to learn till she is married or fit to be so ; and surely these are not to be learned in a school : my next reason is that I am not at all fit for the task. I have seen a good deal of the education of boys, but in a girls' school I should be quite a novice. I never was at one myself, I have not even the advantage of sisters; indeed for the early part of my life, I conversed little with my own sex. In the village where I was there were none to converse with ; and this I am sensible has given me an awkwardness about common things which would make me peculiarly unfit for the education of girls. I could not judge of their music, their dancing ; and if I pretended to correct their air, they might be tempted to smile at my own ; for I know myself to be remarkably deficient in gracefulness of person, in my air and manner—I am sensible the common schools are upon a very bad plan, and believe I could project a better—but I could not execute it."

The rapid and uninterrupted success of
the school was no doubt partly owing to
Mrs. Barbauld's name ; and Mr. Barbauld's
county connections brought them several
sons of noblemen and gentlemen of fortune.
Mrs. B. threw herself heart and soul into
the work. She kept all the accounts (still
extant) of the school and their private purse.
She wrote charming lectures on History and
Geography, and took the entire charge of a
class of little boys. The first Lord Denman,
Sir William Gell, Dr. Sayers, and William
Taylor of Norwich, both well-known writers,
were among these. For them and her nephew Charles she wrote her 'Early Lessons'
and 'Hymns in Prose.' Dr. Johnson and
Mr. Fox were both pleased to express their
disapproval of her wasting her talents in
writing books for children,* but, practically
employed in education as she then was, she
felt the entire want of elementary books fit
to put into their hands, and naturally was
led to try to supply it. Her preface to the

---

* See Boswell's Life of Johnson, and Recollections
of C. J. Fox by Mr. Rogers.

Early Lessons first written for her little Charles explains this.

"This little publication was made for a particular child, but the public is welcome to the use of it. It was found that amidst the multitude of books professedly written for children, there is not one adapted to the comprehension of a child from two to three years old. A grave remark or a connected story however simple is above his capacity, and *nonsense* is always below it, for folly is worse than ignorance. Another defect is the want of *good paper*, a *clear and large type*, and large spaces. Those only who have actually taught young children can be sensible how necessary these assistances are. The eye of a child cannot catch a small obscure ill-formed word amidst a number of others all equally unknown. To supply these deficiencies is the object of this book. The task is humble, but not mean, for to lay the first stone of a noble building and to plant the first idea in a human mind can be no dishonor to any hand."

Of the 'Hymns in Prose for Children,'

perhaps the best known of all her writings,
she says in her preface her "peculiar object
was to impress devotional feelings as early
as possible on the infant mind—to impress
them, by connecting religion with a variety
of sensible objects, with all that he sees, all
he hears, all that affects his young mind
with wonder and delight; and thus by deep,
strong, and permanent associations, to lay
the best foundation for practical devotion
in future life."   That this end was accomplished, the numerous editions, even to the
present time, of this charming little work,
fully shows.

To relieve their minds as much as possible during this busy life, Mr. and Mrs.
Barbauld always spent their winter vacation
in London, and took some journey in the
summer, a few extracts from the letters she
regularly wrote to her brother are here given.

London, Jan., 1784.
" Well my dear brother, here we are in
this busy town, nothing in which (the sight
of friends excepted) has given us so much

pleasure as the sight of the balloon exhibiting in the Pantheon, it is sixteen feet one way and seventeen another. When set loose from the weight, it mounts to the top of that magnificent dome with such an easy motion as puts one in mind of Milton's line, "rose like an exhalation"............Next to the balloon, Miss Burney is the object of public curiosity. I had the pleasure of meeting her yesterday. She is a very unaffected sweet and pleasing young lady— but you, now I think of it, are a Goth, and have not read Cecilia. Read it, read it, for shame !...

I begin to be giddy with the whirl of London, and feel my spirits flag. There are so many drawbacks, from hair dressers, bad weather, and fatigue, that it requires strong health greatly to enjoy being abroad.

We are got into the visiting way here, which I do not consider quite as an idle employment, because it leads to connections, but the hours are intolerably late ; the other day at Mrs. Chapone's, none of the party but ourselves was come at a quarter to eight, and the first lady that arrived said she hurried away from dinner without waiting for coffee. There goes a story of the Duchess of Devonshire, that she said to a tradesman, ' call on me to-morrow morning at four,' and that the honest man knocked the family up at day-break. Last week we met the American Bishops at Mr. Vaughan's, —if bishops they may be called—without title, without diocese, and without lawn sleeves. I wonder our bishops will consecrate them, for they have made very free of the Common Prayer, and have left out two Creeds out of three................................

I have been much pleased with the poems of the Scottish Ploughman, (Burns). His Cotter's Saturday Night has much the same merit as the Schoolmistress ; and the Daisy, and the Mouse, are charming. The Eton Boys have published a periodical which they say is clever.* Dr. Price has a letter from Mr. Howard dated Amsterdam ; he says the Emperor gave him a long audience. A pasquinade was fixed upon the gates of the

* The Philanthropist.

lunatic hospital in Vienna, 'Josephus, ubi-
cumque secundus, hìc primus.'

The King, I heard, was playing at drafts
with Dr. Willis, and having got a man tọ
the top, the Dr. asked ' if he would not *crown
his king.*' 'No' said his Majesty, 'for I
think a king the most miserable man on
earth.'*...

Charles is losing his hair, (after a fever)
I believe I ought to have the rest shaved,
but it is such a frightful thing to see a boy
in a wig. Do you remember some of my
father's scholars in wigs? I do, and coat
lappets set out with buckram. Well, I hope
we do improve in taste...............................

What have you seen, you will say, in
London? Why in the first place Miss
More's new play which fills the house very
well and is pretty generally liked. Miss
More is I assure you very much the ton, and

* Mrs. Barbauld always felt respect and attachment to
the King, partly perhaps from being exactly of the same
age. Her writings seem to have become known at Court,
as her mother, in one of her letters, says " Miss Belsham
has heard that Her Majesty (Queen Charlotte) has declared, that if she is an enthusiast in anything it is in
admiration of Mrs. Barbauld."

moreover has got 600*l* or 700*l* by her play. I wish I could produce one every two winters, we would not keep school. I cannot say however that I cried so much at ' Percy,' as I laughed at the ' School for Scandal ' which is positively the wittiest play I remember to have seen, and I am sorry to add, one of the most immoral and licentious. In principles, I mean, for in language it is very decent.

Mrs. Montagu, not content with being the Queen of literature and elegant society, sets up for the Queen of fashion and splendour. She is building a very fine house, has a fine service of plate, dresses, visits more than ever, and I am afraid will be as much the woman of the world as the philosopher. I heard much of the Astronomer,* who has discovered three hundred new stars and a new planet or comet. He was a piper in a Hessian regiment, and has improved telescopes to an astonishing degree. He has sat they say for twenty-four hours, rubbing and polishing his spectrum, and been

* Herschel.

fed by the attentions of others. We are
reading in idle moments, Boswell's long
expected life of Johnson. It is like going
to Ranelagh, you meet all your acquain-
tances; but it is a base and a mean thing to
bring thus every idle word into judgement;
the judgement of the public. Johnson, I
think, was far from a great character, he
was continually sinning against his conscience, and then afraid of going to Hell for it.
A Christian, and a man of the town; a
philosopher, and a bigot; acknowledging
life to be miserable, and making it more
miserable through fear of death; professing
great distaste to the country, and neglecting
the urbanity of towns; a Jacobite and
pensioned; acknowledged to be a giant in
literature, and yet we do not trace him as
we do Locke, or Rousseau or Voltaire in his
influence on the opinion of the times. We
cannot say, Johnson first opened this view
of thought, led the way to this discovery,
or this turn of thinking. In his style he is
original, and there we can track his imita-
tors.—In short, he rather seems to me to

be one of those who have shone in the belles
lettres, rather than what he is held out to
be by many, an original and deep genius in
investigation. ....

Mrs. Montagu, who entertains all the
aristocrats of France, had invited a Marchioness De Boufflers and her daughter to
dinner —after making her wait till six, the
Marchioness came and made an apology for
her daughter, that just as she was going to
dress she was seized with a 'dégoût momen-
tané du monde,' and could not wait upon her.

Mr. Brand Hollis has sent me an American poem, a regular epic in twelve books—
The Conquest of Canaan—but I hope I need
not read it. Not that the poetry is bad. if
the subject were more interesting. What
had he to do to make Joshua his hero, when
he had Washington of his own growth.

Mr. Howard is setting out upon another
tour to the north-west of England ; he looks
well and happy and lively ; he has been
south as far as Moscow, where he says that
they live in all the Asiatic magnificence.
He told me of a Russian nobleman who has

built a convent, where he has educated at his own expense 600 young ladies, by whose means he hopes to polish the Empire."

A further notice of this great man occurs in a letter about this time, in a letter from Mrs. Barbauld's mother in Warrington. " Mr. Howard left us yesterday to the great regret of all who had the happiness of his acquaintance, he is indeed an astonishing person ; where could another be found who would incur the expense, fatigue and danger which he has done, in visiting three times over every prison in England, besides many in foreign parts ; where, one who has brought his appetites under such subjection as to be able to live almost without eating ? He takes nothing but a dish of tea or coffee and a mouthful of bread and butter till night; and then eats only a few potatoes, and drinks nothing but water, and yet he never seems to want either spirits or strength, and is a most lively entertaining companion." He once told them that wishing, whilst in Paris, to see the Bastille, he made inquiries for that purpose, and finding it quite impossible to obtain an order, he determined to try without one. Accordingly he boldly drove up to the gates in a handsome carriage and four, with several servants in livery, dressed himself like a gentleman of the court. Stepping out of the carriage, with an air of authority, he desired to be shown over the building. The officials, taken by surprise, and never doubting from his deportment his right to be obeyed, permitted him to examine everything he chose. A further short account of him by Lucy Aikin may be introduced here—it was written late in her life to a young relation.

" Few, very few, survive to the present time to say, I remember Howard the ever memorable philanthropist—I have seen him, his image is still before my eyes— a small man, brisk in his movements, with an expressive countenance—extremely fond of children and entertaining them with narratives fitted to their understanding. I was indeed no more than eight years old when his high career was arrested by death, on a

far distant coast, but immediately before
embarking on his last hazardous journey,
he had passed some time where my father
then resided, at Yarmouth in Norfolk, occupied in preparing for the press, with his
assistance, his concluding volume on Laz-
arettoes, Prisons, and Hospitals. He loved
to unbend at times from this occupation, to
forget for a few moments in domestic intercourse the scenes of distress and horror which
he had encountered in the fulfilment of his
high mission, and which he viewed it as a
sacred duty to expose to public notice. The
society of my mother was peculiarly accept-
able to him. Her step-mother was a lady
of the Whitbread family, with which Mr.
Howard was closely connected both by
blood and friendly intercourse, and from
this circumstance she had enjoyed from her
tenderest years, the privilege of knowing and
revering him, whilst her strictness of principle, her steady conduct, and the whole
cast of her serene and amiable character,
had been peculiarly adapted to win his
esteem and affection.

Both in his frequent visits to London, where Arthur Jennings, my grandfather, usually lived, and afterwards in Bedfordshire, where he had inherited a small family estate at Harlington, within a few miles of his own property at Cardington, Mr. Howard had many opportunities of cultivating this family connection, and I conceive this to have been the channel through which my father, the nephew as well as the son-in-law of Mr. Jennings, was introduced to him. It had been the irreparable misfortune of Mr. Howard, owing to the narrow and sordid notions of ignorant guardians, who placed him under an utterly incompetent schoolmaster, never to obtain the power of writing correctly his own language. On this account he had always found it desirable to obtain literary assistance, in giving to the world the valuable matter of his works.

It was under my father's superintendence that his previous volumes had issued from the Warrington Press, and he was now for the last time imparting a precious record of his unparalleled exertions to one who enter-

G

ed heart and soul into his objects, and honored himself almost beyond all human beings."

Eleven years spent in teaching left Mrs. Barbauld, as well as her husband, so much exhausted and out of health, that they gave up their school at the end of that time, in 1785; and after a year spent on the continent and another in London, fixed themselves at Hampstead, where, besides taking one or two pupils, Mr. Barbauld accepted an invitation to perform duty at a small chapel, for which a larger building has now been substituted, and of which the Rev. Dr. Sadler is the minister.

Mrs. Barbauld describes the place in a letter to her brother ;

" Hampstead is certainly the pleasantest village about London. The mall of the place, a kind of terrace, which they call *Prospect Walk*, commands a most extensive and varied view over Middlesex and Berkshire, in which is included, besides many inferior places, the majestic Windsor and lofty Harrow, which last is so conspicuously placed that you know King James called it 'God's visible Church upon earth.' Hampstead and Highgate are mutually objects to each other, and the road between them is delightfully pleasant, lying along Lord Mansfield's fine woods, and the Earl of Southampton's *ferme ornée*. Lady Mansfield and Lady Southampton, I am told, are both admirable dairy-women, and so jealous of each other's fame in that particular, that they have had many heart-burnings, and have once or twice been very near a serious falling-out, on the dispute which of them could make the greatest quantity of butter from such a number of cows. On observing the beautiful smoothness of the turf in some of the fields about this place, I was told, the gentlemen to whom they belonged had them rolled like a garden plot.

I imagine we shall stay here till pretty late in the autumn, but if we enjoy the sunny gleams, we shall likewise endure many a cutting blast, for I think, except Avignon, this is the most windy place I ever was in.

As we have no house, we are not visited
except by those with whom we have connections, but few as they are, they have
filled our time with a continual round of
company, we have not been six days alone.
This is a matter I do not altogether wish,
for they make very long tea drinking after-
noons, and a whole long afternoon is really
a piece of life. However they are very
kind and civil. I am trying to get a little
company in a more improving way, and
have made a party with a young lady to
read Italian together.

I pity the young ladies of Hampstead,
there are several very agreeable ones. One
gentleman in particular has five tall mar-
riageable daughters, and not a single young
man is to be seen in the place, but of
widows and old maids such a plenty."

The village of Hampstead was then even
more secluded than its distance from town
seemed to warrant, the hill apparently being
considered almost inaccessible. In a diary
kept by Mr. Barbauld, he frequently speaks
of being prevented going to town by the

state of the roads; and the passengers by
the stage coach were always required to walk
up the hill.   Mrs. B. in a letter to Dr. Aikin
describes the house they afterwards took as
" standing in the high road at the entrance
of the village quite surrounded by fields."
The house still stands—the one immediately
above Rosslyn Terrace—but the fields have
alas, disappeared.

Mrs. Barbauld found many excellent and
kind friends in this place.   Mrs. Joanna
Baillie, Mr. Hoare, and Mr. and Mrs. Carr
of Frognal were some of the most intimate;
with the last large family she remained on
affectionate terms to the end of her life.
Mr. Carr, then Solicitor to the Excise, was
always ready to give her his valuable legal
advice, and help; and the eldest daughter,
afterwards married to the Rt. Hon. Dr.
Lushington, was her peculiar favorite.

Joanna Baillie and her sister had lately
established themselves also in a house at
Hampstead, in which for the next half
century they received all the choicest society
England could boast—Mrs. Barbauld writes

--" I have received great pleasure lately from the representation of De Montfort, a tragedy which you probably read half a year ago in a volume entitled ' A series of Plays on the Passions.' I admired it then, but little dreamed I was indebted for my entertainment to a young lady of Hampstead whom I visited, and who came to Mr. Barbauld's Chapel all the while with as innocent a face as if she had never written a line. The play is admirably acted by Mrs. Siddons and Kemble, and is finely written, with great purity of sentiment, beauty of diction, strength and originality of character ; but it is open to criticism—I cannot believe such a hatred natural. The affection between the brother and sister is beautifully touched, and as far as I know, quite new. The play is somewhat too good for the present taste."

At Hampstead Mrs. Barbauld wrote several of her prose Essays, and contributed to Dr. Aikin's popular little work of " Evenings at Home "—of which however only fourteen of the ninety-nine pieces are her's. Also a poem addressed to Mr.

Wilberforce on the rejection of the "Bill for abolishing the Slave Trade." Mrs. Hannah More acknowledged a copy of the poem as follows.

Cowslip Green, July, 1791.

My dear Madam,

Sickness and a variety of perplexing circumstances have thrown me so much out of the way of seeing you, that I hardly feel myself intitled to any mark of kindness from you. But had I seen your incomparable Poem by *accident*, and had it *not* come to me endeared as your gift, I should not have been able to have withheld writing to you to express my delight, my gratitude, my admiration. I cannot tell you how many times I have read it. I really had begun to pray (as I told the excellent person to whom you have addressed it) that my poetical enthusiasm was quite dead, but I find that like another idol it was only gone a journey or was asleep, and that it can be awakened at any time by such verses as you have sent me. I thank you for writing so well, for writing on a subject so near my heart, and for addressing it to one so every way worthy of your highest esteem. I could not forbear repeating to him part of the animated description of the union of barbarity and voluptuousness in the West Indian woman, and he did full justice to this striking picture.* He is now upon a visit to me, and I wish I could tempt Mr. Barbauld and you to indulge me with your company...........you would find quiet, pleasing picturesque scenery, a few books and a great deal of friendship.

I hardly know how to enclose the trifling verses within. I wrote them in a playful

---

*Lo ! where reclined, pale Beauty courts the breeze
Diffused on sofas of voluptuous ease;
With anxious awe her menial train around
Catch her faint whispers of half-uttered sound;
See her, in monstrous fellowship unite
At once the Scythian and the Sybarite!
Blending repugnant vices, misallied,
Which frugal nature purposed to divide;
See her, with indolence to fierceness joined,
Of body delicate, infirm of mind,
With languid tones imperious mandates urge;
With arm recumbent wield the household scourge;
And with unruffled mien, and placid sounds,
Contriving torture, and inflicting wounds.

hour at the Bishop's; they owe their appearance in print to the gallantry of my friend Mr. Walpole. To send them to you is keeping up the African trade of beads and bits of glass in exchange for gold and ivory. My sisters join me in kind regards to Mr. B. and yourself,

I am, my dear Madam,
Your obliged and very affectionate,
H. MORE."

The poem mentioned at the end of this letter was called ' Bonner's Ghost ' in which he is supposed to lament the liberality of the age; this drew an answer, which will be found in the Appendix. It was never before printed, but copies must have been circulated, as the lines

"Nor brush one cobweb from St. Paul's
Lest you should shake the dome,"

were quoted in a Church debate in the House of Commons. It is to be supposed she did *not* send a copy to her friend Hannah More.

Between the Aikin and the Rogers family

a long friendship had subsisted, and Mrs. Barbauld watched the career of the young poet* with affectionate interest—he preserved among his papers the following letter—we cannot discover however whether he accepted the invitation it contains, and joined Mrs. Barbauld's party to the Long Room.

" To Mr. Samuel Rogers, junr.

Sir,

We are obliged to you for much elegant amusement, thro' the books which we safely received, and which we shall beg leave to keep a little longer. Your visit was so short that we wish to think of anything which may induce you to make a longer, and

---

*Mr. Rogers has often been accused of too great fondness for rank and fashion, he was however sincerely anxious to become a popular poet, and nothing gratified him more than to think his writings known to the classes below himself. He told Miss Aikin, in illustration of this, that being one evening in the gallery of the Opera House, he observed a plain, very respectable, elderly man gazing at him for a long time with great earnestness. At length, between the acts, this person quitted his seat, and coming up to him said solemnly, " pray sir, is your name Samuel Rogers ?" "Yes, it is," he replied, with a benignant smile. " Then sir, I should be glad to know why you have changed your poulterer."

as we are to have an assembly at the Long
Room, on Monday next, the 22nd, which
they say will be a pretty good one, I take
the liberty to ask whether it will be agreeable to you to be of our party, and in that
case, we have a bed at your service. I
could, I am sure, have my petition supported
by a round robin of the young ladies of
Hampstead, which would act like a spell.
to oblige your attendance, but not being
willing to make use of such compulsory
methods I will only say how much pleasure
it will give to Sir,

Your obliged and obedient servant,
A. L. Barbauld.

Our dinner hour, if you can give us your
company to dinner, is half after three.

Hampstead, October, (about 1788.) ''

In the year 1793 Mrs. Barbauld paid a
visit to Edinburgh, no letters are preserved
describing it, but Sir Walter Scott gives the
following account of an evening at Mr.
Dugald Stewart's, at which he was not
himself present, though he and Mrs.

Barbauld afterwards met in London.

It will be observed that he calls her Miss Aikin though she had been married more than twenty years.

" About the summer of 1793 or 1794, the celebrated Miss Letitia Aikin, better known as Mrs. Barbauld, paid a visit to Edinburgh, and was received by such literary society as the place then boasted, with the hospitality to which her talents and her worth entitled her. Among others, she was kindly welcomed by the late excellent and admired Professor Dugald Stewart, his lady, and family.

It was in their evening society that Miss Aikin drew from her pocket-book a version of ' Lenore ' executed by William Taylor, Esq., of Norwich, with as much freedom as was consistent with great spirit and scrupulous fidelity. She read this composition to the company, who were electrified by the tale. It was the more successful, that Mr. Taylor had boldly copied the imitative harmony of the German, and described the spectral journey in language resembling

that of the original. Bürger had thus
painted the ghastly career.

> ' Und hurre, hurre, hop, hop, hop !
> Ging's fort in sausendem Galopp,
> Dass Ross und Reiter schnoben,
> Und Kies und Funken stoben.'

The words were rendered by the kindred
sounds in English.

> ' Tramp, tramp, across the land they speed,
> Splash, splash, across the sea,
> Hurrah ! the dead can ride apace
> Dost fear to ride with me ?'

When Miss Aikin had finished her reci-
tation she replaced in her pocket-book the
paper from which she had read it, and enjoyed the satisfaction of having made a
strong impression on the hearers, whose
bosoms thrilled yet the deeper as the ballad
was not to be more closely introduced to
them. The author* was not present on this
occasion, although he had then the distinguished advantage of being a familiar friend
and frequent visitor of Professor Stewart
and his family. But he was absent from
town while Miss Aikin was in Edinburgh,

* Sir Walter Scott.

H

and it was not until his return that he found all his friends in rapture with the intelligence and good sense of their visitor, but in particular with the wonderful translation from the German by means of which she had delighted and astonished them. The enthusiastic description given of Bürger's ballad and the broken account of the story, of which only two lines were recollected, inspired the author, who had some acquaintance as has been said, with the German language, and a strong taste for popular poetry, with a desire to see the original."

(From Scott's Essay on Imitations of the Ancient Ballads.)

The only reference found to this visit, is in a letter to her niece Lucy Aikin, who also visited Edinburgh many years later— it is dated from Stoke Newington, December 12th, 1811.

"My dear Niece,

I am much obliged to you for your entertaining letter, indeed we live very

much upon your letters, and as that kind
of food has the property as well as the
widow's cruse of being divided without di-
minishing, we do not scruple to impart it.
I rejoice you spend your time so pleasantly
at Edinburgh, as indeed you could not well
fail to do in such a family and such a town.

I have not yet received from the Princess
Mary˙ her picture set in diamonds, nor a
tea equipage of Sèvres China, nor so much
as a gold medallion of the King, with a
round robin of thanks from all the Royal
family, one or other of which I have been
in daily expectation of ever since I heard
from you Lord Buchan's intention with regard to my poor copy of verses,* which, I
must confess I did not think quite calculated
to please a courtly ear, however, as Lord
Buchan has got them, let him do what he
pleases.—Pray tell him with my compliments, that I have by no means forgotten his
hospitality nor the pleasant day I spent at
Dryburgh Abbey, nor the busts, nor the

---

* On the King's illness.

incident of my hat's falling into the Tweed,
and if he will send me the verses he wrote
on that occasion, I will send him mine on
the ruins of the Abbey............Does Jeffery
ride his great horse yet? By the way, I
wish Grace would draw a caricature of that
scene, where *you* were bridling, Miss
Fletcher I suppose tittering, and the conscious culprit* bowing—or is he where he
ought to be, on his knees at your feet—but
possibly you are very good friends by this
time.

Well I have finished my verses, there are
a hundred and fifty faults in them, more
than I can mend, but my brother is pleased
with them, so I shall have some talk with
friend Richard about it.† I would advise
you to let Constable have the Ode to Dun

---

* Dr.——had been engaged to Miss Aikin; he broke
it off owing to a distrust of his pecuniary resources, which
turned out to be quite unfounded. Meeting her some
years after at Edinburgh, where she was much admired
and caressed, he would gladly have renewed the engagement had Miss A. been so inclined; she was so no longer
however, though they remained good friends to the end
of their lives.

† Mr. Richard Taylor, the printer.

Edin and Holyrood House, and that pretty little piece to Grace Fletcher on her drawing her mother's portrait, which you have written, but send us down some copies by the coach, for I want to see them. How ridiculous the complaint of the Clans you tell me of against Miss Baillie. I suppose it would be taking too great a liberty to write anything about Gog and Magog, lest it should affront some of their descendants.

Pray if you see Miss Maclear give her my affectionate compliments, and to Mr. and Mrs. Dugald Stewart pray express my affectionate veneration. Farewell, tho' we miss you, we do not wish you in any other place or company than that where you are receiving and giving so much pleasure.

Your affectionate aunt,
A. L. BARBAULD."

A letter from Dr. Priestley in his self-imposed banishment in America belongs to this period.

"Northumberland,
United States, 1797.

Dear Mrs. Barbauld,

The pleasure I received from your letter was the greater from it having been unexpected. It has brought a great number of pleasing scenes to mind, tho' attended with the melancholy reflection that one person* present to them all is now absent. Tho' for many years she wrote but few letters, there were not many persons who were more frequently the subject of our conversation, or whom she spoke of with so much pleasure as yourself. Indeed, pleasing impressions of so early a date are not soon effaced, if no pains were taken to revive them. If my diaries had not been destroyed in the riots, I should have been able to retrace some of them better than I can do now. She often lamented the loss of a folio book, into which she had copied all your unpublished poems, and other small pieces, especially the first poem we ever saw of yours, on taking leave of her when we left

* His wife.

Warrington, and of this I think I heard you say you had no copy. The perusal of it would give me more pleasure now than it did at the first. The short and very just character which you draw of her I have, and value much. We regretted also the loss of the little poem you wrote on the birth of Joseph. But the time is fast approaching, with respect to me, when our intercourse, from which I have derived so much satisfaction, will be renewed with advantage; and to this future scene late events have drawn my attention in a more particular manner than ever. How much to be pitied are they who are not Christians. What consolation can they have in their sorrow? mine have sometimes such a mixture of joy as hardly to describe the name.

Your letter, tho' dated Feb. 28th, I have but just received, and since that date I find I am under particular obligations to you for taking under your care a daughter of Sally.* A friend in need, they say, is a friend indeed, and such you are to her, and I consider it

---

* Dr. Priestley's daughter, Mrs. Finch.

as more than any act of friendship to myself.

What you wish *almost*, I wish *altogether*, that you and many others of my friends in England, were here. There cannot be a more delightful spot on the face of the earth, and here I trust we shall have *peace*. In England, I fear, there will be troubles. If possible, however, I propose to myself the satisfaction of seeing my native country once more before I die.

I am glad that what I published here in defence of Christianity, gives you pleasure. By this time you may have seen more pieces of the same tendency. Here the defection from Christian principles is as great as with you. But I consider it a certain sign of better times. I am much pleased with Mr. Towers *on Prophecy*. It is an extraordinary performance for so young a man. I hope that a beginning being now made, our correspondence will be continued, at least occasionally. I shall always be exceedingly happy to hear from you. With all our best respects,   Your's and Mr. Barbauld's,

Most sincerely,

J. PRIESTLEY."

Dr. Aikin who had been for some years established as a physician in London, was in 1798 attacked with an illness which seemed to threaten his life, and put an end to his hopes of remaining in practice. He therefore gave up his house to his son Charles, and took one in Stoke Newington, then a pretty and rural village, of which Lucy Aikin writes, "This suburban village has been a very Elysian field of non-conformity. Worthy Dr. Watts resided here five years from 1876, as tutor to the son of Sir John Hartopp, Bart. The last thirty-six years of his life, which ended in 1748, were also passed here under the roof of first, Sir Thomas Abney, and afterwards of his widow and daughter in succession. Dr. Price lived as domestic chaplain for the thirteen years preceding 1757, with Mr. Streatfield, of Church street, Stoke Newington, in one of the two houses which about 1709 had afforded a tranquil shelter to the memorable Daniel Defoe, also a dissenter.

Here too England's great philanthropist John Howard, born in 1727, resided between 1752 and 1756. On his removal, with characteristic generosity, he made a handsome donation to the congregation in Church street, for the purpose of providing a house for the minister. Here no doubt must have been formed his intimate, confidential, and affectionate friendship, with the excellent Dr. Price, in which he found unfailing aid and solace, down to their last solemn leavetaking, previous to the departure of Howard on his last pilgrimage."

Dr. Aikin, though so ill when he went to Stoke Newington (to which the family were drawn by its being the abode of Mrs. Kinder, Mrs. Aikin's only sister,) recovered, and really lived twenty years there; giving himself to a life of literature, but occasionally practising in consultation, and attending many poor persons gratuitously.

Between himself and his sister the tenderest affection had always existed, and the longing for daily intercourse now became so strong in both, that Mrs. Barbauld in 1802 persuaded her husband to quit Hampstead and purchase a house close to her brother's, in which she remained to the end of her life. A little poem addressed to her by her brother, at this time expresses their feelings.

Yet one dear wish still struggles in my breast,
And points one darling object unpossest ;—
How many years have whirled their rapid course
Since we, sole streamlets from one honored source,
In fond affection as in blood allied,
Have wandered devious from each other's side ;
Allowed to catch alone some transient view,
Scarce long enough to think the vision true !
O then while yet of life some zest remains,
While transport yet can swell the beating veins,
While sweet remembrance keeps her wonted seat,
And fancy still retains some genial heat ;
When evening bids each busy task be o'er,
Once let us meet again, to part no more !

The following letters belong to this time. They are arranged according to dates. The literary project, mentioned by Miss Edgeworth, in the first letter, does not appear to have ever been carried out.

July 22nd, 1804.

" My dear Madam,

I will not trouble you with any common places, about time, and distance, and friendship, but taking it for granted that you are the same Mrs. Barbauld, and that I am the same Maria E. who made acquaintance with each other in the year 1799, I proceed to mention a scheme of my father's. He thinks that a periodical paper, to be written entirely by ladies, would succeed, and we wish that all the literary ladies of the present day might be invited to take a share in it.—No papers to be rejected—each to be signed by the initial of the author's name—each to be inserted in the order in which it is received.

If you approve, tell us what would be the best method of proceeding. Would a paper in the Monthly Magazine put the business in train ? Why cannot you, dear Mrs Barbauld, prevail upon yourself to come to Ireland, or rather, why cannot *we* prevail upon you ? We do not pretend to diminish the terrors of sea-sickness, but we could hope to balance a few hours of pain by some months of pleasure. We are vain enough to feel tolerably certain that you would be happy in the midst of a family, united amongst themselves, who have from their childhood, heard the name of Mrs. Barbauld with respect, and who, as they have grown up, have learnt better and better to appreciate her merit.

Mrs. Edgeworth and my father join with me in every kind wish for your health and happiness, and we hope we have not lost our place in good Mr. Barbauld's esteem and affection. Believe me to be, my dear madam,

Your sincerely affectionate,
MARIA EDGEWORTH."

" Stoke Newington,
Aug. 30th, 1804.

Dear Madam,

I wish I could convey to you an adequate idea of the pleasure it gave me to receive a letter from your hand, and I will add, of the sensibility excited in me by that

I

token of your esteem, conscious as I was
that my own hand had but ill obeyed the
dictates of my heart, in expressing those
sentiments of esteem and regard which are
indelibly engraven upon it. When I received
your letter I was just going to Tunbridge,
and as the contents required some consideration, I thought it best not to answer it
till my return. As to the scheme of a periodical paper, there is no one who would not
be delighted to see it undertaken by yourself and *Co.*, provided the *Co.* was in any
measure adequate to the first of the firm,
but I do not know what to say to the idea,
which seems to be a leading one in your
plan, of inviting the literary ladies to join
it. All the literary ladies! Mercy on us!
Have you ever reckoned up how many there
are, or computed how much trash, and how
many discordant materials would be poured
in from such a general invitation. I feel
also doubtful of the propriety of making it
declaredly a *lady's paper*. There is no bond
of union among literary women, any more
than among literary men; different senti-

ments and different connections separate
them much more than the joint interest of
their sex would unite them. Mrs. Hannah
More would not write along with you or me,
and we should probably hesitate at joining
Miss Hays, or if she were living, Mrs.
Godwin. But suppose a sufficient number
willing and able to co-operate, which I am
willing to think might probably be found,
still I do not see why it should be ostensibly
'The Lady's Paper.' Many would sneer
at the title, they would pretend to expect,
however unreasonably, frivolity or romance.
There is a great difference between a paper
written *by* a lady, and *as* a lady. To write
professedly as a female junto seems in some
measure to suggest a certain cast of sentiment, and you would write in trammels.
If a number of clergymen were to join in
writing a paper, I think they should not
call it '*The Clergymen's Paper*,' except they
meant to make it chiefly theological. With
regard to the scheme in general of a periodical paper, I am apt to think there is
room for one. *The Mirror*, and Cumber-

land's *Observer* were the last of the kind, if
indeed they may be reckoned of the kind.
The Mirror was never circulated in England
but in vols., and I am not sure whether the
Observer was anywhere. A paper is a
pleasing mode of writing, as it admits equally the lightest and the gravest subjects ; the
most desultory, and the most profound, if
treated concisely ; but humour and character, the manners and modes of the times,
seem to be the subject more particularly
called for. And why if you can find gentlemen, should not gentlemen be admitted.
I am sure we have not any writer of that
sex who ought not, and I believe who would
not, be proud to join with Miss Edgeworth;
and surely Mr. Edgeworth at least would
give his assistance, and would not Dr.
Beddoes ? How rich an accession that
would be. One thing my own judgment is
clear in, that there ought not to be more
than half-a-dozen principals in such a
scheme, occasional correspondence should
also be admitted, but by no means without
selection, and a very strict one too, other-

wise you would be overwhelmed with trash ;
and if you print in London, the person who
selects must live there, and perhaps the
same person as Editor should have the care
of the paper, so far that it should be on him
or her to see that the press did not stand
still. I should think signatures, that might
be afterwards acknowledged like those in
the Spectator, would in general be more
agreeable to the feelings of the writers than
the giving the name at first. With regard
to myself, I would offer you my assistance,
and should feel highly gratified in all respects if you permitted me to join my name
with yours, did I feel that fertility and flow
of fancy which is requisite for the undertaking. Once it was a favorite scheme of
mine, had my brother been willing to join,
and I had then several little pieces which
might have answered such a purpose, but
they have been scattered about in Magazines, and I dare not trust to the future,
expecting naturally to grow duller and duller,
and besides always writing slow, so that I
should not dare to bring upon myself an

obligation, I should feel a tremendous one, that of supplying the press at stated times, whether I have anything to say or not—but I would rank with pleasure among the occasional contributors, If I can be of any service by sounding or inviting anybody that I know in London, male or female, to the scheme, command me. We have here Miss Baillie, Mrs. Opie, give me leave to add my niece Lucy Aikin, and many others; Mr. S. Rogers I rather think would not be averse to join a scheme of this kind. But you—you are a host in yourself. How much have we all to thank you for of entertainment and instruction, how admirably have you contrived to join fancy, interest, knowledge of the world, sound sense, useful morality in the various pieces which with so rich and flowing a vein of instruction you have poured out before us. Will you permit me to name my two favorites in your last work. They are *Rosanna* and *To-morrow*, tho' the latter I confess I read not without some twinges of conscience which interrupted my amusement...............

I am told just now I ought to be frightened at the impending invasion, and if I were at a watering place perhaps I should, but really the invasion has been *got up* so often it begins to lose its effect, and I think we are pretty well prepared; besides my being afraid will do no good.

Remember us to Mr. and Mrs. Edgeworth with affection and gratitude, and may every happiness rest on yourself and your family is the wish of Mr. Barbauld and myself."

To Mrs. Barbauld,

" Edgeworthstown,
September 4th 1804.

My dear Madam,

I tell you, because I know it will give you pleasure, that no people in similar situations upon this oblate spheroid which used formerly to be called a globe, live together in more perfect amity and confidence than Mrs. E., Maria, and myself, and yet till this day I never ventured to open a letter directed to either of them. But this morning, as Maria's literary partner, I took it upon my conscience and honour to open yours in her absence, as I knew your hand and as I was privy to the contents of her letter to you. She will take great pleasure in returning an answer of her own; but that shall not prevent me from seizing this favourable occasion of assuring you of my most sincere and affectionate esteem, and of the regard and respect which I feel for Mr. Barbauld.

I agree with you implicitly in all you say with respect to my scheme for a Feminead. It is something curious that the subject and the title should be spoken of in Mr. Edwards' letters to Richardson, which came to our hands long after Maria had written to you.

In particular I agree with you about the imprudence of engaging to furnish, as poor Johnson was obliged to do, a certain quantity of copy every week. To avoid this necessity nothing is requisite but such a collection of papers as would suffice for two thirds of the work before we published any. To prevent all cavil as to female authorship—let the paper be announced as the work of a society of Gentlemen and Ladies. Bankers, I mean honest, solvent bankers, keep two-thirds of whatever may be demanded from them in constant readiness, we may therefore not only collect two-thirds of the original stock, but each of the society may engage to furnish one additional paper as soon as one of their writing has been published.— The editor would thus be tolerably secure of sufficient support.

The names you mention are highly approved of in this family. Miss Baillie has more of what is usually called genius than most ladies whose works have fallen into my hands. The correctness, sound judgment, and enlarged mind of another female writer, who has still more genius, might be acquired by Miss B. if she is a lady who supposes that those who write and act the best are those who are most capable of improvement. I do not know Mrs. Inchbald, but my son Lovell (who is still prisoner at Verdun) thought well of her; would she be a useful

correspondent ? We are so unfortunate as
never to have seen Miss Aikin's poetry for
children; but we saw one piece of her writing in London five years ago, and we saw
the lady herself. We are therefore able to
determine that she does not disgrace the
Aikin school.

We have read the greatest part of
Richardson's Life and Correspondence.
Your criticisms are excellent, and your
censures of the indecent passages in your
author are highly becoming and highly
useful. As your sex becomes more civiliz-
ed every day, it is necessary that they should
become more circumspect in conversation
and in all the paraphernalia of modesty.
A married lady in France is allowed one
lover, she is pardon'd for two; three is rather
too many—but great delicacy of sentiment,
elegant language, decent dress, and a good
choice of the objects of her attachments will
preserve her from absolute excommunica-
tion, but a failure in any of these circumstances places her in a disreputable class of
females. You have made R. appear to

great advantage, without using any of the unfaithful arts of an editor. You have shewn, that like other mortals, he had failings; but his enthusiasm for virtue, his generosity, and true politeness of heart and conduct, are brought so distinctly before the eye, that we love the man as much as we admire the author. His invitations to his friends are so kind and so hearty, that we really wish to learn his art of persuading those whom he loved to visit him, and we would try it first upon you. If the French land in England, which I think will happen, come over here, where you may be sure they will not come till they have tried their fortune on the shores of Britain.

We have learned some good precepts from your criticisms, and in return I have mark'd two or three careless passages in the early part of your life of Richardson. I took the book out of the hands of one of the eight readers round our table this 4th of September, 1804, 9 p.m., to look for some of my criticisms, but I was so struck upon the second reading with your excellent remarks

upon Pamela, that I could not turn away to
look for them, and the book could not be
spared to me. Why do you quote Sedley's
lines, they are un peu trop séduisants. I
am delighted with Mad. Klopstock, and absolutely shocked at her death. Richardson's
remarks on Miss Mulso's correspondence
about love are of high value, particularly to
us, as they are the best apologies I have
seen for Belinda—whom Madam de Sanza
(formerly Mlle. Flacoux) thought a monster,
not a woman.

Mrs. E's. daughter, whom she was nurs-
ing when you saw her, caught something of
the divine air from your kisses. She
promises to have an observing judicious
mind and an affectionate temper. She has
two other daughters—none of them beauties
—but all very well—all healthy. I have a
charming daughter— a most promising lad
of science, ten years old—and two fine
captains, who will defend and amuse you if
you come here—but nobody here or elsewhere values you more highly than I do.

Be so good as to give my respects to Dr.

Aikin who supports virtue, science, and good
letters, so ably by his pen and his example.

I am, Dr. Madam,

Most sincerely yours,

R. L. EDGEWORTH."

" Edgeworthstown,

Sept. 23rd, 1804,

My dear Madam,

On my return home yesterday I
had the pleasure of your letter; my father
would not forward it to me, but kept it, as
he said, on purpose to increase my agreeable
associations with home. It was indeed a
great pleasure to receive such a letter from
you. From the first moment that you pro-
fessed a regard for us, I never could doubt
of our holding a place in your esteem, so
long as we remained unchanged; but notwithstanding the steadiness of this belief,
it was delightful to me to receive assurances
under your own hand and seal that I was
in the right. The freedom and affectionate
warmth of your letter were peculiarly grateful to me; and though the praise you bestow

K

on some of our works, may be far beyond
what your cool judgment would allow, yet
I am perfectly well satisfied to find that in
our cause your judgment is not cool. Is not
it said of Pascal, that he wore a girdle of
spikes, which he pressed into himself whenever he was conscious of any emotions of
vanity ? How deep they must have been
pressed, if he had been praised by Mrs.
Barbauld ! For my part, I do not pretend
to any ascetic humility, nor do I inflict upon
myself the penance of abstinence from the
refined delicacies of praise—especially when
they are presented by a friend.

With respect to *the Lady's Paper*, my father
desires me to tell you, dear Madam, that it
was his proposal, not mine ; I am glad that
your objections have appeared to him satis-
factory. I agree with you perfectly in
thinking that to provoke a war with the
other sex, would be neither politic nor becoming in ours. Our literature should never
be placed in competition with theirs to
plague them, it should be added to the
common stock of amusement and happiness.

To attempt to form a corps of literary women, where all would wish to be officers, except those best suited to command, where there would be no discipline, and where, as you observe, the individuals might not choose to mess together, would be absurd and ridiculous.

As I was not at home, when my father answered your letter, I am perhaps repeating the very things which he has said; but this you must excuse, for we are notorious for expressing the same ideas, often in the same words, at different ends of the same room.

To one thing in your letter, dear Madam, I must object, even if my father has not dared to do so : I must remonstrate against your being only an occasional correspondent. I am not surprised, that you should not like to bind yourself to feed the press with daily delicacies, but by proper economy and arrangements, amongst the principal purveyors, you would never be exposed to this tremendous necessity. I hope therefore that upon *second thoughts*, which Dr. Aikin will in this case allow to be best, you will consent to give credit to our *firm*, by placing your name foremost as the acting partner. We should rejoice to have the able, and elegant assistance of Miss Aikin, of your brother, and of Mr. Rogers, Miss Baillie, and Mrs. Opie.

Do not imagine, dear Mrs. Barbauld, when I mention the life of Richardson, that I am going to attempt that return of eulogium, with which authors sometimes treat each other.—You are quite above this traffic of bays, and, I hope, so am I. The eager interest with which I read the life of Richardson you would have thought the most unequivocal testimony I could give of my liking it. My father, in jest, said that I was wildly anxious to read it, because it was the life of an author, but I knew that my interest in it arose from its being written by Mrs. Barbauld. I think I should be able to distinguish her style from that of any other female writer by the ease, frequency, and felicity, of its classical allusions —allusions sufficiently intelligible to the unlearned, and which serve as freemason signs to the learned.

Though you have such an aversion to the sea, we do not yet give up the hopes of having you and Mr. Barbauld at Edgeworthstown. We shall expect you along with the blessings of peace. But when— is I fear in the bosom of Emperors. In the mean time, dear madam, accept my grateful thanks for your kindness, and believe me with sincere esteem and admiration.

Affectionately yours,
MARIA EDGEWORTH."

" Stoke Newington,
January 28th, 1805.

Dear Miss Edgeworth,

I appear before you again as a culprit, and you have too much reason to imagine me inattentive to the contents of your last most friendly letter. They have however dwelt much upon my mind, and when I returned home (for I received it at Bristol) I revolved the scheme much in my

mind, and made what enquiries I could of
the probable success of a periodical paper,
and it should seem that the first step should
be to consult with a Bookseller, for tho'
there would be no doubt of the success when
gathered into volumes, there is no very
recent experience of an undertaking of this
kind in the *feuille volante*. The *Mirrors* were
never published in England, till they were
in volumes ; and the *Ramblers*, as I see from
Richardson's correspondence, lay heavy on
Cave's hands when they first came out.
Therefore the opinion of a Bookseller should
be first had, and that Bookseller should be
a man, active, and disposed to push such a
scheme, not to let the papers sleep in his
shop for want of advertisements, &c. Then
as to the coadjutors, as it is no longer
necessary they should be all ladies, I have
been this long while attacking my brother
on the subject, but on account of his other
engagements, I cannot get him to think of
more than an occasional paper, which I dare
say he would now and then offer. There is
a person, whom I should think very proper

for such an undertaking, and I think it not unlikely that it might suit him, as, with a good deal of genius, he has not, that I know of, any important literary work in hand; I mean Mr. William Taylor of Norwich. He has an uncommon share of learning and information, and great originality of thought and style; the last mentioned quality it is necessary to apprise you of, because it often leads him to singularity both in matter and style, and I believe he often sports opinions for the value of defending them, with a great deal of ingenuity and critical acumen. In language, he is fond of old Saxon words, thinking, and very justly, that we have weakened the nerve and strength of our language, by abandoning much of its ancient riches, But he *can* write without these particularities. He has written a good deal of poetry, which ought, I think, to have established his fame, but it has been carelessly thrown into Magazines, piece by piece, and has not assumed that importance to the eye, which is generally necessary to give celebrity. Perhaps you may have seen

his translation (the best I think) of Bürger's
Leonora; and a beautiful one of Goethe's
Iphigenia. As a man, he is most amiable
and worthy. I was on the point of mentioning the scheme to him, but I thought it
was right *you* should first know what he was.
But, my dear Madam, I am convinced it is
necessary for such a scheme as this, that
you should yourself come to town, and in
truth you ought to do so on every account.
We cannot let Ireland engross you. Come
and enjoy your own celebrity. Come and
give pleasure to your numerous friends.
Come and explore all London can afford of·
food for the mind and the imagination. In
two or three years there is always something
new. How much I should rejoice in such
a determination, I trust I need not say,
nor how much I shall feel myself honoured
and delighted with as much as you can
afford me of your society. I became very
impatient for your *Griselda*, before Johnson
thought proper to produce it, need I add we
have read it with great pleasure. It is
charming, like everything you write, but I

can tell you the gentlemen like it better than the ladies, and if you were to be tried by a jury of your own sex, I do not know what punishment you might be sentenced to, for having betrayed their cause. " The author is one of your own sex, we men have nothing to do but to stand by and laugh ;" was the remark of a gentleman, no less candid aman than Dr. Aikin: and then the moral (a general moral if I understand it right), that a man must not indulge his wife too much! If I were a new-married woman, I do not know whether I would forgive you till you had made the amende honorable, by writing something to expose the men. All however are unanimous in admiring the sprightliness of the dialogue, and the ingenious and varied perversenesses of the heroine. The Royal Institution has been very much crowded this year, and Sidney Smith is the favourite of the day. I have not heard him, but I understand he makes his lectures on morals very *diverting*, which is not exactly what I should have expected from such a subject, however, it succeeds. Have you seen Master Betty? have you heard Sidney Smith? are the questions that generally succeed one another. We enjoyed great pleasure this summer in seeing your two sisters at Bristol, and in being introduced to Mr. King, whom we had not seen before. And now, if I were not so near the bottom of my paper, I should turn to Mr. Edgeworth, and thank him for the favour of a charming letter, which, if I possessed a share of his sprightliness, I would endeavour to answer. I am very sensible to the obliging things you both say on the subject of Richardson, and I kiss the rod with regard to the verses of Sedley. To own the truth, my conscience did remonstrate a little, but I was seduced by the beauty of the verses. Seriously however I shall be much obliged to Mr. Edgeworth or you for any criticisms on the *life*, because Phillips talks of publishing it separately. I am obliged to comprise in little room a thousand things, as well from Mr. Barbauld as myself, which would endeavour to express the esteem and affection so justly due to

Mr. and Mrs. Edgeworth and all your family.
Believe me ever, with high regard.
Yours &c.,
A. L. BARBAULD."

To Miss Aikin,
At Mr. Taylor's, Norwich.
" My dear Niece,
After the very entertaining letter
you favoured me with, you had a right
to expect an earlier answer, and nothing,
believe me, has prevented it, but the con-
ciousness of not having equal entertainment
to offer in return.

I am much obliged to you for the information relative to the convenience of our
good friends with regard to receiving us,
but I do not now think we shall take the
journey at all this year, for I am grown so
deaf of late, that I am not willing to intrude
such an infirmity on the sprightly and animating parties Norwich affords, or to
undergo myself the mortification of Tanta-
lus, when the cup of social joy is offered to
my lips. I rejoice however in the pleasure

that you are giving and receiving, and most
particularly in the good accounts of your
health, the foundation of all enjoyment.
I hope this journey will strengthen and
confirm it, and that every circumstance
will contribute to increase the pleasure we
shall enjoy, when we see you again. We
have paid two pleasant visits since I heard
from you, one was to Mr. Rogers in his
elegant house, looking into the Green Park,
every decoration of which is as elegant and
recherché as his verses. Indeed, I think one
might naturally conclude from the perusal
of his poems, that his bookcase is of satin-
wood, and his drawing room furnished with
marbles, bronzes, &c. The company was
Mrs. Weddel a connoiseur in painting and
an intimate friend of the late Mr. Palgrave,
Gifford, Mathias, the Rogers', and Sharpes,
and Mr. S.—distinguished in the witty and
fashionable world, and whose conversation
is esteemed by his admirers the most brilliant of any man's in those circles. There is
a romantic story belonging to his marriage.
When abroad in Italy, he unconsiously, as

it is said, made a conquest of the heart of a married lady. Her husband, who doted upon her, discovered his wife's attachment, I believe indeed she acknowledged it to him, upon which he wrote to Mr. S. who had then left the place, to meet him at a town which he named. Mr. S. went and found the corpse of the husband, who had shot himself, and a letter in which he said that finding Mr. S. alone could make his wife happy, he had taken out of the way the only impediment to their union and charged him as a man of honour to marry and protect his wife. And could she marry him upon her husband's grave said I? But Mr. Barbauld asserts she was obliged to it from regard to her husband, who otherwise would have shot himself thro' the head for nothing. I leave it as a crust for the female casuists. Well, our other visit was paid yesterday to Dr. Gregory* (or *parson* G. as his parishioners call him) and his wife at West Ham. My brother and sister were with

---

* Rector of West Ham, and husband to a dear old friend of Mrs. Barbauld's.

L

us. We called in the way on Mr. Lindsay who has got a very noble house indeed by Old Ford, which situation lying under some suspicion from the neighbourhood of the Lea marshes, Mr. Macmurdo stoutly asserted that the playground was as high as St. Paul's. West Ham betrays its vicinity by a plantation of reeds for the basket makers, and causeways raised above the meadows, and as a village it is inferior to Layton—however our friends like it, they have got a good house and Mrs. Gregory seems quite happy with the varied employments of visiting the parish, taking care of her children, pigs, ducks, peacocks, cows, &c., &c.; she assures me she can make butter.

We have been reading with might and main to get thro' Mr. Roscoe's four 4to vols.; for four 4to vols., let me tell you, is an arduous undertaking; and there is such an utter depravity of morals, and all kind of principles among these Italians, that there is hardly one I care three farthings about. I was struck with one passage as affording a fine frame for a novel in the gloomy and terrible style to be entitled *The Confessions of Gonsalvo*. Gonsalvo, it seems, on his death-bed lamented two faults he had been guilty of in the course of his life; but there was a third crime he never would reveal, 'he *could* have unfolded a tale' says Roscoe, but he died a penitent, and trusted it with his other faults to the bosom of his God. Now he *must* have revealed it to his Confessor who might have committed it to writing and it was probably found by the French, in some of the late convulsions, from whence Mr. Godwin, I think, might come to the knowledge of this mysterious and horrible crime. Or will you and Mr. Taylor undertake it? But I believe your conferences are rather metaphysical, and if so, pray Madam what is your opinion of *causation*? Do you agree with Dugald Stewart, Hume, and Mr. Leslie, because if you do, I think you may as well throw Paley's last work into the fire. But perhaps you are by this time got to Yarmouth, and if so, I fear you are out of the way of enjoying and giving pleasure. Wherever you are, pray remember us to those we

know and love. To Mr. Taylor and dear
Susan, I will certainly write soon. There
is only one sentence of your letter I quarrel
with, where you *apologize* for large paper.
Fie! Repeat the fault and I will forgive
the apology. All are well and desire to be
remembered.

Your affectionate aunt,
A. L. BARBAULD.

Stoke Newington,
 July 27th, 1805."

" Edgeworthstown,
Feb. 26th, 1806.

My dear Mrs. Barbauld,
   Holcroft wrote the heads of the
Chapters in Popular Tales; he was employed by Johnson to correct the press. We were
so much *scandalized* when we saw them that
Johnson offered to cancel the whole impression. My father says that I should not
enter into long explanations about trifles;
but I cannot help being anxious to assure.
you, that those trite vulgar sentences were

not written by my father and preceptor.
You will wonder why I should thus abruptly
address my justification to you. My dear
Madam, we have just been reading a review,
or rather an eulogium of Popular Tales,
which from the excellence of the writing
and its generous warmth, we are persuaded
could be written by no other but our friend
Mrs. Barbauld. I never felt, and my father
declares he never felt, so much pleasure from
any praise—indeed we never before received
any of so high value and from a judge whom
we so much respect. We would rather
have one grain of such praise than a cwt.
of compliment from common critics.

I regret that I inserted in the Modern
Griselda the offensive line from Chaucer.
Let me assure you that this little tale was
written in playfulness not bitterness of
heart. My father had often declared that
he could not be imposed upon by me; but
that he should know my writing without
my name to it. When he was absent for a
few weeks, and none but the *ladies* of the
family at home, I wrote this story, sent it to

L 2

Johnson, had it printed with a title page
without my name, and on my father's return home showed it to him. Not one of
the female committee who sat upon it every
day whilst it was writing and reading ever
imagined that it would be thought a severe
libel upon the sex—perhaps because their
attention was fixed upon Mrs. Granby, who
is at least as much a panegyric as Mrs.
Bolingbroke is a satire upon the sex. It is
curious that the Edinburgh Reviewers laugh
at us for introducing into every story some
charming wife, sister, mother, or daughter,
who acts the part of the good fairy of the
piece. Leonora will confirm them in this
opinion and will I hope make my peace with
you.

There is some probability that my father
and two or three of this family may be in
England this year, and we look forward to
the hopes of seeing you, my dear Madam, as
one of the greatest pleasures that a visit to
London can afford. My brother Sneyd,
who is going to enter the Temple, will certainly accompany my father to England.

You may remember, if you do not always
forget your own goodness, that you select-
ed and read to us, several years ago, some
lines *On Evening* in the Monthly Mag. by
C. S. E.—written when he was ten years
old. He has not indulged since in writing
much poetry as he had far other studies to
pursue for the College of Dublin—on quit-
ing that College he wished to leave some
memorial behind, and he has just finished a
poem called *The ' Transmigrations of Indur '*
—the plan taken from your tale in Evenings
at Home. If this poem should obtain a
premium from the College we shall think
it worthy of the honor of being presented
to you my dear Mrs. Barbauld.

My father did not see you since he saw
Mr. and Mrs. Carr in Bloomsbury Square :
they were extremely civil to him, and im-
pressed him with the idea that they would
be inclined to comply with any reasonable
request that he might make to them. My
father wishes for Mr. Carr's advice as to
the best method of disposing of Sneyd in
London for two years to come. It is his

present intention to be called to the Irish bar, and two years will be sufficient eating for him, to complete his terms, as he has already eaten nine terms in Dublin. If Mr. Carr could afford five minutes to write to him he would esteem it a real favour.

He wants his advice at present, simply on these questions—

Where should Sneyd *lodge* ? And what mode of *living* whould he recommend ?

Mrs. Edgeworth and my father are as anxious as I am to preserve a place in Mr. Barbauld's benevolent heart. My father hopes he is now quite well.

Believe me, dear Mrs. Barbauld, I am with sincere esteem and grateful affection,
Your friend,
MARIA EDGEWORTH."

To Miss Edgeworth,
" Stoke Newington,
March 23rd, 1806.

Dear Madam,

Few things, believe me, can give me greater pleasure than to be remembered by you with that partiality which you have indulged me with. To read you, to hear from you, and to see you, makes up the most agreeable climax in the world, and I am truly delighted to find that we on this side the water may hope to enjoy the last part of it. But I was much surprised to see your letter begin with the name of Holcroft. How, thought I, can Holcroft come in as a third between Miss Edgeworth and me? To be serious, I do assure you upon my honour, that I did *not write* the Review of Popular Tales,* nor did I see a single word of it till I received the printed vol. Nor did I ever review any work of yours. I am also of opinion that the manner in which the titles were mentioned, was not sufficiently respectful to Mr. Edgeworth, even supposing him the author, and that it was very little necessary to mention them at all. For my own part I am not sure that I knew there were titles till Mr. Edgeworth directed my attention towards them, for when a building is very inviting I am but

* It was written by Lucy Aikin.

little inclined to stop at the porch. And
now, my dear Miss Edgeworth, permit me
to ask whether it is not more regular to
address any remarks relative to a Review
to the *Editor*, who is the only ostensible
person in the business. I do assure you I
have never asked, nor do I know, the
Reviewer of any article of mine in the
Annual R., tho' the Editor is my own Nephew. And now let me thank you for the
very high pleasure and entertainment we
have recently received from your Leonora,
the heroine is an amiable and touching
picture of every virtue, and if there are any
who think you have played false to our sex
in Griselda, I hope they will be satisfied
with the *amende honorable* you have made
them. If I were writing to any one but
yourself, I should say more than you would
perhaps allow me to, of the delicate satire,
the good sense and knowledge of life, the
wit and brilliancy displayed in the characters of Olivia and Gabrielle, that admirable
Gabrielle, so truly a Frenchwoman, so
characteristic, and yet, till you drew her,

not that I know of, described. And the
General's letters! But I forbear. There
is however in all human compositions something for a critic to nibble at, and if I have
the pleasure of seeing you, I shall ask you
whether you believe a promise binding upon
the conscience, that cannot be kept without
a crime, an engagement to one person that
implies the breach of a previous solemn vow
to another. It is impossible, I think, such
a sentiment can be yours, yet is not the
reader led to think so? Extricate me my
dear Friend from this difficulty. Pray have
you seen a small vol. of Poems by Mr. Montgomery?* We are all delighted with them,
and consider him as a new star risen on the
poetical horizon. The author is a printer
at Sheffield, and has made himself what he
is, and seems to have keenly felt, as all in
narrow circumstances must do, the mortification of having his mind ill suited to his
situation and his prospects. There is a
poem in particular, entitled *the Ocean*, very
striking, both from its sentiments and its

* James Montgomery.

harmony. A verse of it has been running in my head all day, as the Park and Tower Guns were firing for our late victory.—

For Britannia is wielding her trident to-day,
And consuming her foes in her ire ;
She is hurling her thunders with absolute sway,
From her wave-ruling chariots of fire.

I have sent Mr. Edgeworth's Queries to Mr. Carr, from whom I suppose he has heard or will hear. I think it is since Mr. E. saw him that Mr. Carr has got the place of Solicitor of Excise. I hope in any case we shall see Mr. Sneyd's Poem when he comes to town. The subject seems to me susceptible of much poetical embellishment. We are impatient to know when you come to London, and how many of the family will be of the party; I would have all, I would not willingly spare one of you to stay at home. When the new projected Balloons are perfected, how pleasantly a family party might come over in one. I have only one word to say, indulge us at Newington as much as you can with your much valued company. In the mean time, present from

Mr. Barbauld and myself, the most cordial and respectful remembrances to Mr. and Mrs. Edgeworth and all the family, and believe me, with the highest sentiments of esteem, Dear Madam,

Your obliged and faithful,

A. L. BARBAULD.

———◆———

MR. BARBAULD's increasing mental disease at this time, made his wife constantly feel the comfort of living close to her brother and his family—though it was not till her life was actually endangered by his violence, that she would consent to any restraint being put upon the unhappy sufferer. He one day at dinner, seized a knife from the table and pursued her round the room; she only escaped by springing from the window

M

into the garden, and taking refuge in Dr. Aikin's house.*   In the end, a separation took place, and Mr. Barbauld was, in the care of a keeper, removed to a house next Mr. C. R. Aikin's, in London, where he seemed for a time to mend.   Being, however, imprudently trusted with money, he one day bribed his attendant to allow him to walk out alone, and as he never returned, search was made, and his lifeless body found in the New River.   Miss Aikin remarks "and though the escape of a sufferer, from the most melancholy of human maladies, could not in itself be a subject of rational regret, her spirits were deeply wounded both by the

---

* It was singular that Mrs. B. ran another danger from the same cause a few years later.

In Mr. Robinson's diary he gives an interesting account of Mr. Elton Hamond, a young man of great talents, eloquence, and remarkably fine person. He came to Mrs. B. with an introduction from the Edgeworths, and was a very frequent visitor, indeed, he persuaded her to take his sister as an inmate for several years.   After a time he became very strange, and in the end destroyed himself.   Mr. Robinson, whom he left his executor, found after his death, among his papers, one which discussed at great length, the best way of '*putting an end to Mrs. Barbauld's life*'—by poison, a sudden blow, shooting, stabbing, &c.

severe trials through which she had passed,
and by the mournful void, which always
succeeds the removal of an object of long and
deep, however painful, interest. An affect-
ing Dirge was found among her poems
which records her feelings on this occasion."

Pure spirit! O where art thou now!
O whisper to my soul!
O let some soothing thought of thee
This bitter grief controul!

T'is not for thee the tears I shed,
Thy sufferings now are o'er;
The sea is calm, the tempest past,
On that eternal shore.

No more the storms that wrecked thy peace,
Shall tear that gentle breast,
Nor Summer's rage, nor Winter's cold,
Thy poor, poor frame molest.

Thy peace is sealed, thy rest is sure,
My sorrows are to come;
Awhile I weep and linger here,
Then follow to the tomb.

And is the awful veil withdrawn
That shrouds from mortal eyes,
In deep impenetrable gloom,
The secrets of the skies?

O, in some dream of visioned bliss,
Some trance of rapture show
Where, on the bosom of thy God,
Thou rest'st from human woe!

Thence may thy pure devotion's flame
On me, on me descend;
To me thy strong aspiring hopes,
Thy faith, thy fervour lend.

Let these my lonely path illume,
And teach my weakened mind
To welcome all that's left of good,
To all that's lost resigned.

Farewell! with honour, peace, and love,
Be thy dear memory blest!
Thou hast no tears for me to shed,
When I too am at rest.

The following extract from a letter of Sir
James Mackintosh to Mrs. John Taylor of
Norwich, must have reached England after
Mr. Barbauld's tragical end. It cannot now
be known whether it was ever seen by the
mourner; but it may be taken for granted,
that so kind and faithful a friend as Mrs.
Taylor, would have communicated anything
that might have soothed her feelings at
such a time of distress.

"Bombay, 10th Oct., 1808.

If I had been a little more acquainted with
Mrs. Barbauld, I should have written to
her.* If I could have spoken any consolation, it would have been only payment of
a long arrear of instruction and pleasure for
thirty years. In another sense, it would
have been but the payment of a debt. I
could have said little, but what I learned
from herself. If ever there was a writer
whose wisdom is made to be useful in the
time of need, it is Mrs. Barbauld. No
moralist has ever more exactly touched the
point of the greatest practicable purity,
without being lost in exaggeration or sink-
ing into meanness. She has cultivated a
philosophy which will raise and animate
her, without refining it to that degree, when
it is no longer applicable to the gross pur-
poses of human life, and when it is too apt
to evaporate in hypocrisy and ostentation.
Her observations on the moral of 'Clarissa,'

* On the aberration of intellect, under which her
husband was then suffering.

M 2

are as fine a piece of mitigated and rational
stoicism as our language can boast of : and
she who has so beautifully taught us the folly
of inconsistent expectations and complaints,
can never want practical wisdom under the
sharpest calamities. Mental disease is perhaps the subject on which topics of consolation are the most difficult to be managed.
Yet I have been engaged since my arrival
here in a very singular and not altogether
unsuccessful correspondence with poor Hall,
formerly of Cambridge, on the subject of
his own insanity. With Mrs. B's firmer
and calmer philosophy, I should think it
easy to teach the imagination habitually to
consider the evil only as a bodily disease,
of which the mental disturbance is a mere
symptom. That this habit deprives insanity of its mysterious horrors, is obvious
enough from the instance of febrile delirium,
which fills us with no more horror than
any other morbid appearance, because we
steadily and constantly consider it as an
effect. The horrible character of the disease
seems much to depend on its being consid-

ered as arising from some secret and mysterious change in the mind, which, by a sort of noble superstition, is exalted above vulgar corporeal organs. Whoever firmly regards it as the result of physical causes, will spare themselves much of this horror, and acquire the means of being useful to the sufferer. My advice may be useless, but I should wish my sympathy known to Mrs. Barbauld. It is the privilege of such excellent writers, to command the sympathy of the distant and unborn. It is a delightful part of their fame; and no writer is more entitled to it, than Mrs. Barbauld."

Mrs. Barbauld had the fortitude to seek relief from dejection in literary occupation, and incapable, as yet, of any stronger effort, she consented to edit in 1810, a collection of British Novelists, with an introductory essay, and biographical and critical notices prefixed to each author.

In the following year, she compiled for the use of young ladies, a collection of verse and prose in one volume, entitled the Female Speaker. She also resumed her correspondence with a few friends; some letters are given here.

To Mrs. Taylor.
"June 18th, 1810.

A thousand thanks for your kind letter; still more for the very short visit that preceded it—though short—too short, it has left indelible impressions on my mind;

my heart has truly had communion with
yours—your sympathy has been balm to it;
and I feel that there is no one *now* on earth
to whom I could pour out that heart more
readily, I may say so readily, as to yourself.
Very good also has my dear amiable Mrs.
Beecroft been to me, whose lively sweetness
and agreeable conversation, has at times,
won me to forget that my heart is heavy.

I am now sitting alone again, and feel
like a person who has been sitting by a
cheerful fire, not sensible at the time of the
temperature of the air, but the fire removed,
he finds the season is still *winter*. Day after
day passes, and I do not know what to do
with my time, my mind has no energy, nor
power of application. I can tell you, however, what I have done with some hours of
it, which have been agreeably employed in
reading Mrs. Montagu's Letters. I think
her nephew has made a very agreeable
present to the public; and I was greatly
edified to see them printed in modest octavo,
with Mrs. Montagu's sweet face (for it is a
very pretty face) at the head. They cer-

tainly show a very extraordinary mind, full
of wit, and also of deep thought, and sound
judgement. She seems to have liked, not a
little, to divert herself with the odd and the
ludicrous, and shows herself, in the earlier
letters, passionately fond of races and balls :
this was natural enough at eighteen. Perhaps you may not so easily pardon her for
having early settled her mind, as she
evidently had, not to marry except for an
establishment. This seems to show a want
of some of those fine feelings, that one expects in youth ; but when it is considered
that she was the daughter of a country
gentleman with a large family, and no
fortune to expect, and her connections all
in high life, one is disposed to pardon her,
especially as, I dare say, she would never
have married a fool or a profligate. I heard
her say—what I suppose very few can say—
that she never was in love in her life. Many
of the letters are in fact essays ; and I think
had she turned her thoughts to write in
that way, she would have excelled Johnson.

I have also turned over Lamb's Speci-

mens of Old Plays, and am much pleased
with them. I made a discovery there, that
La Motte's fable of Genius, Virtue, and
Reputation, which has been so much
praised for its ingenious turn, is borrowed
from Webster, an author of the age of
Shakespeare; or they have taken it from
some common source, for a Frenchman was
not very likely to light upon an English
poet of that age : they knew about as much
of us then, as we did, fifty years ago, of the
Germans. It is surprising how little invention there is in the world ; no *very* good
story was ever invented. It is perhaps
originally some fact a little enlarged,
then by some other hand embellished with
circumstances, then by somebody else,
a century after, refined, drawn to a point,
and furnished with a moral. When shall
we see the moral of the world's great story,
which astonishes by its events, interests by
the numerous agents it puts in motion, but
of which we cannot understand the bearings, or predict the catastrophe ? It is a
tangled web, of which we have not the clue.

I do not know how to rejoice at this victory, splendid as it is, over Buonaparte, when I consider the horrible waste of life, the mass of misery, which such gigantic combats must occasion. I will think no more of it; let me rather contemplate your family; there the different threads all wind evenly, smoothly, and brightly."

To Miss Edgeworth.
" Stoke Newington,
September 5th, 1809.

My dear Madam,

I am much obliged to you for your permission to enrich the Selection of Novels with your ' Belinda ' and ' Griselda,' and am quite of your opinion that the latter answers more truly to the definition than ' Castle Rackrent,' the high merit of which has given me a desire to lay hands upon it, as writers sometimes will strain a point to enrol a favorite character among their countrymen. I remember Mr. Senebier, in his account of the illustrious men of Geneva, reckons, first, those who were born and lived

there; then those who were born in the
territory, but lived elsewhere; thirdly, those
who lived at Geneva and were born in other
countries, and, lastly, some of those if very
eminent, who had made any *occasional stay*
in the place. I mention it, that if you
have a particular objection to be claimed by
future generations for any country province
you may take care not to go there. But to
return to my Novels, from which I confess
I have rambled somewhat unreasonably.
As you wish them to be printed from your
corrected copy, the Booksellers will be much
obliged to you to send one as soon as may
be convenient, as they wish now to set
about printing in good earnest. To say the
truth, the whole ought to have been out
long ago, but the course of my thoughts
and my whole mind has been so adverse
for many months past, which you will not
wonder at, to the engagement I had entered into, that I have sufficiently exercised
the forbearance of the Booksellers. Let me
now, my dear Miss Edgeworth, thank you
for the very great pleasure which, in com-

mon with all who read, I have received from your new tales. I may not, to you, expatiate on the variety, the invention, the spirit, ever new and ever charming, of your various publications, but I may congratulate you on having so much power, and so much will to impress the heart with virtuous feelings, and by those modes of writing which are generally managed so as to enfeeble the mind, to gird it up for the real business and duties of life You may expect some striking Poetry soon from Montgomery,* I do not know whether he is a favourite of yours. I think Campbell has disappointed the public in his Gertrude, and I doubt if he will ever recover his ground. You know I presume, that Miss Hamond is with me, and I am gratified to find that she seems to be happy, as it also contributes to my comfort that I have one with me to break the solitude of my desolate house. I saw her brother yesterday, the high respect all the family have for you makes an interesting point of connexion between us. Miss

---

* James Montgomery.

Hamond says modestly that *she* is not your correspondent, and therefore hardly thought herself entitled to send her respects. I told her I should send them notwithstanding, and I have now not room for more than to add mine to Mr. and Mrs. Edgeworth, whose kindness I know. I am a poor correspondent, but should you ever feel inclined to bestow a line upon me, it would give me true pleasure. My Brother's family desires remembrances."

To Mrs. Barbauld.

" Edgeworthstown,

January 18th, 1810.

My dear Madam,

I have great pleasure in making a good beginning of this new year by fulfilling a request of your's. My brother Sneyd will have the honor of waiting upon you with 'Belinda.' I wish I could be of the party, but alas! this is quite out of my power. My father, thank God, has perfectly recovered his health and strength, but he is now engaged in an undertaking which will attach him for some time to the bogs of Ireland.

Sneyd will give you an account of the
Commissioners for improving our bogs;
and pray ask him for a history of the moving
bog in our neighbourhood, of the wonders
of which he has been an eye witness. I
would tell you of these, but that he can tell
in five minutes what I could not write in
five. So to return to my own business.
'Belinda' I have taken some, and my father
has taken a great deal of pains, to improve
her. In the first volume, the alterations
are very slight, and merely verbal. In the
second volume, '*Jackson*' is substituted for
the husband of Lucy instead of '*Juba*,'
many people having been scandalised at the
idea of a black man marrying a white
woman; my father says that gentlemen have
horrors upon this subject, and would draw
conclusions very unfavorable to a female
writer who appeared to recommend such
unions; as I do not understand the subject, I trust to his better judgment, and
end with—for Juba read Jackson.

In the third volume, I have taken out
everything that gave encouragement (be-

yond esteem) to Mr. Vincent, for great
complaints were made against Belinda for
want of constancy to Clarence Hervey, and
for jilting Vincent. By taking out her
consent to marry, I hope I shall in some
degree, satisfy all parties. Belinda is but
an uninteresting personage after all, but I
cannot *mend* her in this respect, without
making her over again—and indeed without making the whole book over again.
I was not either in Belinda or Leonora
sufficiently aware that the *goodness* of a
heroine interests only in proportion to the
perils and trials to which it is exposed.

I have been made still more sensible of
my own deficiencies, by just reading the
' Simple Story,' which throughout has such
a powerful, irresistible, interest. I hope you
think of it as I do, that it is one of the most
pathetic tales that ever was written.

I long, my dear madam, to see your
prefaces * and wish for your sake as well as
for that of the public, that they were finished;
for I know how any unfulfilled engagement

* To Mrs. Barbauld's Edition of the British Novelists.

of that sort presses upon the mind.

What a loss, what an irreparable loss we have had of our excellent friend Johnson ;* ask Sneyd to tell you how generously, how kindly, he behaved to us in the last act almost of his life. I think the excellent character of him which appeared in the Star could have come from none but such a writer and such a friend as Mrs. Barbauld. I am glad to hear that Johnson's habits of liberality did not injure his fortune, and that his property descends to a representative so worthy of him as Mr. Miles. Ask Sneyd also how Mr. Miles behaved towards us. I know you have pleasure in hearing of instances of virtue in whatever class or rank of life.

I do not know whether you received a letter I wrote you some time ago, about a son of Mrs. Priscilla Wakefield, Mr. Edward W. who has spent some time with us. The idle stories which have been in circulation about him and which originated, as I firmly believe, only in the imprudence or malice of some young ladies have died away, and

* Mr. Johnson the Publisher.

people are coming round to our opinion of
him. I wish to have this supported however by your testimony in his favour.

I beg you will say every thing that is
kind for me to Miss H. Hamond, who I hope
continues with you, that is the best wish I
can form for her improvement and happiness. I hope her brother is well, and
engaged in some fixed pursuit, commercial
or literary or both. Mrs. Edgeworth and
my father beg their kind respects to you.

Believe me, dear Madam,

Your obliged and affectionate

MARIA EDGEWORTH."

1810.

" Dear Miss Edgeworth,

I feel myself very faulty towards
you in not having written before, when I
have many things to thank you for, and
many things to say. It has in part been
owing to the expecting the corrected copy
of 'Griselda,' as it has not been sent, I
imagine you have no corrections to make,
and I find the Printers, without my know-

ledge, have presumed so far on that
supposition as to proceed to the printing,
but they desired me to say they would
cancel anything you wished, if they have
notice time enough. I hope however you
have no alterations, I am sure I cannot
discern that it wants any. We have read
with great pleasure Mr. Edgeworth's work.*
You and he, who are all candour, encourage
me to criticise it, and had I felt that I had
anything to offer which would be of service,
I might have been presumptuous enough to
attempt the task, but indeed I had not.
There is only one passage which struck me
as particularly objectionable in the detail,
that is partly obviated by a note, and in
another Edition Mr. Edgeworth will probably alter it in such a manner as to prevent
misconstruction. You will perhaps guess
that I mean the passage where the Gauls
(as I recollect, I have not the book to refer
to) are mentioned as exciting the courage
of their youth by allowing them to torment
their prisoners. But tho' my penny arrows

---

* Practical Education.

of criticism, if I were inclined to shoot them,
would recoil blunted and harmless against
the book considered as a composition, I do
not say that I can quite agree with the
author with respect to the leading idea, the
devoting a child from its birth to a particular profession. I fear the expectations of
the present would be often disappointed,
from the alteration in his own circumstances
which fifteen or sixteen years is likely to
produce; few ever remain in the same
position, except gentlemen of estates for
that space of time, they are richer or poorer,
they have changed their residences and got
into other connections, a relation will introduce their child into his business, &c.
How can a young couple entering life, with
their fortune to make, uncertain of success
and whether their family be large or small,
devote from its birth, their first child to any
particular profession. They can only determine, as they generally do, that it shall
be very clever and very successful and rise
very high in whatever it undertakes. The
cradle is rocked by Hope, but her bright

visions can scarcely take any determinate
form. Then with regard to the child, his
health, the gradual development of his
faculties, impressions made accidentally will
favour or counteract the views of his parents,
and circumstances will operate over which
they have no controul. A friend of mine
says she is sure her son was determined to
the law by seeing Counsellor Mingay, who
lived next door to them, coming home every
evening with his green bag, which he
imagined was full of money. I should be
afraid also, where the plan succeeded, of
producing a regard too exclusive for a particular walk of life. I should have supposed
the paths of life did not divide so soon.
Let the young colt run freely about for a
while before the blinkers are put on, which
must, alas, when he is put to real service
confine his eyes to one unvarying straight-
forward path, for the remainder of his life.

But from all these saucy remarks which
you have encouraged me to make on the
work of one so infinitely better acquainted
with life and manners than myself, do you

conclude that I wish the book unwritten or altered? Certainly not. In this as in all great questions let men of abilities write, and write strongly, on the side that strikes them; by this collision the truth will be struck out. A part of a system is often practicable where the whole may not be so, and the reader, from various views of various authors, strikes out a medium which would be insipid in the authors themselves, but may best suit his particular case. Alas! how have we been disappointed on this side the water by the failure of your proposed expedition to England. How fondly did I cherish the hopes of seeing you; I will foster the idea that it is only delayed, and I hope the state of Mr. Edgeworth's health will allow me to do so. Everybody here has been reading with great avidity 'The Lady of the Lake,' and there are two parties about it. One that extol it above anything the author has written, another that pretends it is made up of shreds and patches from his former poems. For my own part I pretend not to decide whether it exceeds or

falls short of the fancy of his former Poems,
but I am sure it has most beautiful passages,
and I admire the fertility of genius and the
wonderful rapidity with which, in so short
a period, he has poured out three Poems of
so much bulk as well as beauty. Have you
read my Niece's Poem ?* I dare venture to
predict that you will be pleased with it, and
I hope the gentlemen will allow that the
partiality of a woman to her sex has not
led her to assume more importance for them
than fairly belongs to them.

She begins to feel a little of the trepidation
about the Reviews, very natural in a young
author, but you, my dear Miss Edgeworth,
I hope, feel yourself quite above them.
You cannot be judged by them, *they* may be
judged by their strictures upon you. I had
not seen the Quarterly before you mentioned it. I then read it with great indignation
indeed, nor could I help venting a little of
it, as much as I thought would do good, in
a paper, which perhaps you saw in the

---

* Epistles on Women by Lucy Aikin.

Gentleman's Magazine. Write on, shine out, and defy them."

"Edgeworthstown,
August 1st, 1810.

My dear Mrs. Barbauld,
Your kind and delightful letter gave us all peculiar pleasure, not only from its kindness and the highly gratifying expressions of a regard, which we *know to be sincere,* but from its proving to us that your mind has resumed all its energy, and that you have recovered from that cruel and unavoidable depression of spirits. You can hardly know unless you were with us, my dear Mrs. B., how much we rejoiced at this, nor how earnestly we desire to add, if we could, to your happiness. Why cannot you cross this vile sea, and be with us in a week? Look at the frank of this letter. With pride I bid you look and see that it is franked by your pupil Lord Selkirk, a pupil who does you the greatest honor, a pupil who sets you the best example too, for this

o

is his second visit to Edgeworthstown.—
And you!

Lord Selkirk begs me to remember him
to you in the most respectful and kind
manner, and I am sure you will be glad to
hear that he seems in perfect health and
happiness. His arrival, and that of a succession of visitors, prevented my finishing
the errata for Griselda as soon as I wished,
and must now be my apology for sending
them to you in their blotted and blurred
state, for I really have not time this day to
copy them, and I fear to delay your printer.

Your observations on Professional Education, are as solid as they are elegantly
expressed. My father thanks you for them
with his whole head and heart. He is
correcting the book for a second Edition,
and he will avail himself of your remarks
about the impossibility in some classes of
life of the parents early deciding the child's
profession.

I thank you my kind and able defender
for the essay in the Gentleman's Magazine.
May it ever be my fate to be so attacked

and so defended. We did not know the Essay was written by you, but the moment we read it we were struck, not only with its strength and ability, but with its judicious zeal, and we settled that it must be written by some *friend* who was warmly and personally interested for us.

Can you suppose that any one in this house could see an advertisement of a book of Miss Aikin's without immediately sending for it ? But alas! you little know how long it is before our impatience to see new publications can be gratified. In the centre of Ireland we wait sometimes months before we can get possession of the books we long for. We have not yet the Lady of the Lake *of our own*, though we have begged and borrowed her, and though we wrote for her the moment we heard that she was about to appear in the world. For 'Epistles on Women' we wrote at the same time, and again, and again, and again! And now we have forbid Sneyd, who is coming over, to appear before us, unless he brings it with him, or unless he sends it (as I have desired him till I am hoarse) under cover, to Edward Connor, Esq., Dublin Castle. What has prevented his doing this, I cannot imagine, and really wish I could beat him for it.

We have not yet given up all hopes of seeing you in England. My father talks of going to London in spring, but I dare not feed my fancy on these 'pictured tales of bright heroic deeds.' I know this however, for certain, that if we do reach London ever again, nothing *can* prevent our having the pleasure of seeing you, and hearing you. My father has quite recovered his health, and is as busy in the vast Hibernian bogs as possible. I don't know whether he will improve *them*, but I am sure they have improved *him*, for the air and exercise have quite renovated him. Mrs. Edgeworth sends her real love to you, which I assure you, she never sends, as words of course, to any body. She is again in blooming health, and her darling little Francis repays her for all she has suffered for him. He has all his father's liveliness of look and quick-

ness of motion, and he is without exception,
the best humored little mortal of his years,
of his months I mean, that I ever saw. He
is now *crowing* and dancing at the window,
looking out at his sisters who are making
hay. I am much inclined to believe that
he has a natural genius—for happiness—in
other words, as Sydney Smith would say,
great hereditary ' constitutional joy.'

I am very well, and have been very idle
lately, but intend to be industrious. I have
however begun a story on *Patronage* and
wish I could talk with you about it for half
an hour or even five minutes. It is so vast
a subject that it flounders about in my hands
and overpowers me. I have also written a
preface and notes (for I too will be an editor)
for a little book which a very worthy country-
woman of mine is going to publish—Mrs.
Leadbeater, grand-daughter to Burke's first
preceptor—She is poor—She has behaved
most handsomely about some letters of
Burke's to her grand-father and herself.
It would have been advantageous to her to
publish them, but as Mrs. Burke (Heaven

knows why) objected, she desisted. The
Bishop of Meath afterwards persuaded Mrs.
B. that the letters w^d be highly honorable
to Burke's memory, and Mrs. B. retracted
and gave her permission, but Mrs. Leadbeater, who is a very scrupulous quaker,
conceived that having once *promised* not to
publish them during Mrs. Burke's life, she
should not break this promise. This
perhaps is a foolish delicacy but it is a fault
on the right side. The book she is now
going to publish, ' Cottage Dialogues,' will
be, I hope, for Ireland, what the Cottagers
of Glenburnie are for Scotland—*minus* the
humor of the cottagers. I do not pretend to
say that the dialogues are equal in humor or
ability to Mrs. Hamilton's book, but I think
they will do as much good in this country
as her's did in Scotland. And they give
such an excellent picture of the modes of
living of the lower Irish, that I am in hopes
they will interest in England. Of this she,
poor modest simple creature, had not the
least hope or idea till we suggested it. We
took her M.S. out of the hands of an Irish

publisher, and our excellent friend's worthy
successor in St. Paul's Church Yard has on
our recommendation agreed to publish it for
her. She accepts from me a preface and
notes for the mere English reader.

Adieu my dear Mrs. Barbauld, abruptly,
but most sincerely, and affectionately,

Your obliged,

MARIA EDGEWORTH."

It was soon after her removal to Stoke
Newington that Mrs. Barbauld made the
acquaintance of one whose active kindness
and animated and interesting conversation
brightened many of her lonely hours. Mr.
Henry Crabb Robinson's own characteristic
account of his introduction to her is given
here.

" I formed a new acquaintance of which
I was reasonably proud and in the recollection of which I still rejoice. At Hackney I
saw repeatedly Miss Wakefield, a charming
girl (eldest daughter of the Rev. Gilbert
Wakefield,) and one day at a party where
Mrs. Barbauld had been the subject of con-

versation, and I had spoken of her in
enthusiastic terms, Miss Wakefield came to
me and said 'Would you like to know Mrs.
Barbauld?' I exclaimed 'you might as well
ask me whéther I should like to know the
Angel Gabriel!' 'Mrs. Barbauld is however much more accessible, I will introduce
you to her nephew.' She then called to
Charles Aikin whom she soon after married;
and he said 'I dine every Sunday with my
aunt at Stoke Newington, and I am expected
always to bring a friend with me. Two
knives and forks are laid for me. Will you
go with me next Sunday?' Gladly ac-
ceding to the proposal, I had the good
fortune to make myself agreeable, and
soon became intimate in the house. Mrs.
Barbauld bore the remains of great personal
beauty. She had a brilliant complexion,
light hair, blue eyes, a small and elegant
figure, and her manners were very agreeable,
with something of the generation then
departing. She received me very kindly,
spoke of my aunt, and said she had once
slept at my father's house. Mrs. Barbauld

is so well known by her writings that it is
needless for me to attempt to characterize
her. In the estimation of Wordsworth she
was the first of our literary women, and he
was not bribed to this judgement by any
especial congeniality of feeling. I may here
relate an anecdote connecting her and
Wordsworth, though out of its proper time
by many years; but it is so good that it
ought to be preserved from oblivion.

It was after her death, that Lucy Aikin
published Mrs. Barbauld's works, of which
I gave a copy to Miss Wordsworth. Among
the poems, is a stanza on Life,* written in
extreme old age. It had delighted my sister, to whom I repeated it on her deathbed.
It was long after I gave these works to Miss
Wordsworth, that her brother said, 'Repeat
me that stanza by Mrs. Barbauld.' I did so.
He made me repeat it again; and so he
learned it by heart. He was at the time
walking in his sitting room, at Rydal, with
his hands behind him, and I heard him
mutter to himself 'I am not in the habit

---

* In the Appendix.

of grudging people their good things, but I
wish I had written those lines.'

Life, we've been long together
Through pleasant and through cloudy weather."

Mr. Robinson also mentions taking
Wordsworth to meet Mrs. Barbauld at a
party at Mr. C. R. Aikin's, at which, though
rather a large one, he himself and the
hostess* were the only persons in the room
who were not authors.   He at another time
took his friend Charles Lamb† and his sister

---

* Her daughter may be allowed here to record the
opinion passed upon her by Mr. Wordsworth, in writing
to Mr. Robinson.   " I have never been well since that
evening, yet I am content to pay this price for the
knowledge of so pleasing a person as Mrs. Charles
Aikin, being quite an enthusiast, when I find a woman
whose countenance and manners are what a woman's
ought to be."
Her family lost her soon after, by a rapid attack of
fever, leaving them desolate, and her youngest child an
unweaned infant.

† Another friend of Mr. Robinson's, an enthusiastic
young American, came one day with a letter of introduction.   He was shewn, for a few minutes, into a
room where the table was laid for dinner, and wishing
to preserve some memorial of his visit, he took some
salt out of a saltcellar, and put it into his pocket.   He
repeated this anecdote himself at Dr. Aikin's, when
Mrs. A., who was rather deaf, understood him to say,
he had put the *saltcellar* into his pocket, which being

to spend an afternoon with Mrs. Barbauld.
She, as well as Dr. Aikin and his daughter,
did early justice to Lamb's genius.

------◆------

At the end of the year 1811, a very
gloomy period, Mrs. Barbauld wrote a poem
bearing that name, which unfortunately
reflected too much of the despondency of
her own mind, and drew down many severe
remarks, notwithstanding the beauty of the
verse. Mr. Robinson says "Dear Mrs.
Barbauld this year incurred great reproach,
by writing a poem entitled 1811. It
prophesies that on some future day, a
traveller from the Antipodes will, from a
broken arch of Blackfriars' Bridge, contem-

---

a rather handsome old-fashioned silver one, she was
filled with wonder at this trait of American manners,
till her mistake being happily discovered, was rectified,
amid the merriment of the party.

plate the ruin of St. Pauls.* This was
written more in sorrow than in anger; but
there was a disheartening and even gloomy
tone, which I, even with all my love for
her, could not quite excuse. It provoked
a very coarse review in the Quarterly, which
many years after, Murray told me, he was
more ashamed of than any other article in
the review."

---

* Mr. Robinson must have had in his mind a similar
passage in Macaulay's works, but the following is an
extract from Mrs. Barbauld's Poem "1811". Must not
this have suggested Lord Macaulay's celebrated "New
Zealander" on the ruined arch of Blackfriars' Bridge?

"Yet then the ingenuous youth whom Fancy fires
With pictured glories of illustrious sires,
With duteous zeal, their pilgrimage shall take,
From the Blue Mountains, or Ontario's Lake;
With fond adoring steps to press the sod
By statesmen, sages, poets, heroes trod.
* * * * * * *
But who, their mingled feelings shall pursue,
When London's faded glories rise to view?
* * * * * * *
Pensive and thoughtful shall the wanderers greet
Each splendid square, and still, untrodden street;
Or of some crumbling turret, mined by time,
The broken stairs with perilous step shall climb,
Thence stretch their view the wide horizon round,
By scattered hamlets trace its ancient bound,
And choked no more with fleets, fair Thames survey
Through reeds and sedge, pursue his idle way."

Miss Edgeworth says, "I cannot describe to you the indignation, or rather the disgust, that we felt at the manner in which you are treated in the Quarterly Review, so ungentlemanlike, so unjust, so insolent a review I never read. My father and I, in the moment of provocation, snatched up our pens to answer it, but a minute's reflection convinced us, that silent contempt is the best answer—that we should not suppose it possible, that it can hurt anybody with the generous British public, but the reviewers themselves. The lines even which they have picked out with most malicious intent, are excellent, and speak for themselves. But it is not their criticism on your poem which incenses me, it is the odious tone in which they dare to speak of the most respectable and elegant female writer that England can boast. The public, the *public* will do you justice!"

This was the last time she appeared in print. No one indeed, who loved her, could have wished her to be again exposed to such a shock to her feelings, or such cruel misunderstanding of her sentiments. The remainder of her life was passed quietly at Stoke Newington, among her family and a few friends. From her nephew Charles, she received all the duty and affection of a son, and in the great sorrow of his life, her kindness to him and his motherless children, was unremitting.

One of the few journies she again took, was to her old friends Dr. and Mrs. Estlin, near Bristol, from whose house she visited Mrs. Hannah More.

She writes to Dr. Aikin.

Bristol.

" Dear Brother,

I thank you for your kind letter, and hope soon to return to the dear circle, for indeed it is quite time I should turn my thoughts homeward. I cannot, however, at present fix the day, but I believe it will be the latter end of next week. Mr. Belsham, I have reason to think, will not come into this part of the country, and my friends here will not let me go without some acquaintance.

We continue to have very fine weather here. It has rained one evening and the ensuing night, and I think that is all the rain we have had since I came here. We had a very pleasant day last Monday at Ham Green. Mr. Bright has greatly enlarged the house, and done it with so much judgment, that you do not perceive it was not all built at once, and he has opened the view, so that you see the river and the vessels from the drawing room. I wished my sister there to see a fine magnolia in full bloom, with many other fine plants and trees. The finest plants, however, are the olive branches round his table, there seems to be the greatest confidence and harmony through all the family. Miss Bright is a very excellent young woman, and employs herself very much among the poor. There is an abominable practice here, which is that of building high stone walls, by way of enclosure, which shut out the view from the road; this they have done great part of the way to Mr. Bright's.

You ask me how my visit to Mrs. More's

went off. Very pleasantly indeed. Nothing could be more friendly than their reception, and nothing more charming than their situation. An extensive view over the Mendip hills is in front of their house, with the pretty view of Wrington. Their house (cottage, because it is thatched,) stands on the declivity of a rising ground, which they have planted and made quite a little paradise. The five sisters, all good old maids, have lived together these fifty years, without any break having been made in their little community, by death, or any other cause of separation. Hannah More is a good deal broken by illness, but possesses fully her powers of conversation, and her vivacity. We exchanged riddles like the wise men of old. I was given to understand she is writing something. Hannah had read with great pleasure your Selden and Usher, and thought it very *liberal*.

I have had great pleasure in congratulating my good friends here, on a legacy of three thousand pounds, which has been left them by an old scholar. John Estlin too has five hundred. Dr. Stock, five thousand.

I hope you will go on with your plan of Biography. I like it much, and here is a subject for you in Bristol; a Quaker, Mr. Reynolds, who they say gives away ten thousand a year; he lives very plainly himself.

Love to the Kinders and my sister.

Your ever affectionately
A. L. BARBAULD."

To Miss Edgeworth.
"Stoke Newington,
August 23rd, 1816.

Dear Madam,

Will you permit me to address you, conscious as I am, that I have neglected the advantage and the honour of that intercourse by letter, which my heart all the while acknowledged in its fullest extent. What an excellent and what a cruel piece is your ' To-morrow !' How you could enter so well into feelings which your activity and strength of mind must have hindered you from partaking, I cannot imagine, but

P 2

to me it has given many a twinge of conscience, and most particularly in the affair
of letter writing which, if I have happened
to delay a little too long, always becomes
difficult to me beyond imagination, Days
pass, and the more honour and esteem I
have for my correspondent, the more I feel
that I have nothing worth communicating
and my brain feels dry, *as the remaining
biscuit after a voyage.* With regard to yourself, though longing to write, I doubt if I
should have had the courage, but for a hint
communicated by Mrs. Joanna Baillie
intimating that I might have taken amiss
not seeing more of you when you were in
London. Oh my dear Miss Edgeworth, I
cannot bear you should think so for a moment. Much as I value your society, I well
know the demands on your time, I know
the homage paid you and I exulted in it
for your sake and for my sex's sake. And
now will you forgive me? Will you now
receive all the acknowledgment I owe you,
both in common with all those who have
been delighted and instructed by your

charming works, and more particularly as
having received them from your hands.
Long may you continue to delight the
world with livelier wit and humour than
those who write merely for amusement, and
with juster and more impressive sentiments
of morality than most of those who write
merely for instruction. I should ask you
if you could resist the general spirit of
migration and stay at home when England
is pouring itself over the continent, if I did
not hear, and very sorry I am to hear it,
that Mr. Edgeworth's state of health is
such as must prevent your leaving him.
I tremble to think what tours must be preparing for the press, what sweeping
characters of nations will be given by the
traveller who has dined two or three times
at a table d'hôte, and how often we shall be
sick between Dover and Calais. I am
wishing to lay a tax on English Absentees,
not the tourist of a few months, but the
Nobleman who dismisses his servants, shuts
up his mansion, and spends his vast rents
abroad. Pray have you any summer in

Ireland ? We have not ; a sweeping, chilling, hope disappointing summer, if we must call it such, but that it might not entirely want energy, we have had, it seems, an earthquake in Scotland. A summer without heat, is like a youth without affections, there is nothing to cheer the damp and dreary season which succeeds it. I have myself felt much want of sóme enlivening influence, to counteract the langour of age, and the dreariness of a solitary house. Writing anything I have not felt equal to, and reading has at times been a task to me, but at present I feel better. Every one here has not been so idle. Perhaps you have seen my brother's *Annals*, and though necessarily somewhat dry, from the necessary compression of such an eventful period, I think you will have been pleased with the fairness and impartiality, with which they are written. My niece, Miss Aikin, has made some progress in her ' Memoirs of the Reign of Queen Elizabeth.' She is taking great pains with it, and I hope it will answer her expectation and her friends'.

We are expecting every day another Canto of 'Childe Harold,' but I apprehend the author has lost too much of the public favour, by his late cruel behaviour to his wife, to be as popular as he has been. I have now upon my table, the strangest Poem 'Wilson's City of the Plague,' a heap of horrors, natural and moral; and 'Leigh Hunt's Rimini,' the most fantastic. Thus it is, when the natural and easy, has become a beaten path, and the intellectual taste wants excitement, as the sensitive, by more pungent, relishes the originally disagreeable. My dear Madam, have I not tired you? Will you forgive me? Will you love me, little as I may deserve it? Will you convey my respectful compliments to Mr. and Mrs. Edgeworth, and best wishes for all your family, and will you believe me, with the highest esteem, and most affectionate good wishes.

Your ever obliged,
A. L. BARBAULD.

I beg you to believe that I have written this upon the 'knees of my heart.' "

To Mrs. Barbauld.

1816.

"My dear Madam,

My sight has lately been so much impaired, as to prevent me from writing with my own hand; I have, however, such a number of good secretaries, as to prevent me from feeling much inconvenience from this circumstance; and I now and then derive a peculiar pleasure in using my pen, upon some extraordinary occasion, to assure a friend of the continuance of my regard. Maria is very timid:—though she ought to have been satisfied, as I was, with the consciousness of feeling undiminished affection and esteem for you. She feared that you might have been hurt, by the hurried manner in which she saw you at Newington.

You were too wise, and too kind, to attribute the shortness of her visit, to any thing but necessity. Indeed the tenor of our lives shows that we value the friendship of the wise and good, instead of courting the notice of the great. In London we certainly met a most flattering reception;

but it has not tempted us to renew our visit. We are perfectly happy in absolute retirement, and we have not the least desire to rush into the continental vortex.

Your letter, my dear Madam, gave me a kind of satisfaction, that is perhaps allied to vanity; but it was a proof of what I have often asserted that ' I never lost a friend in my life.'

I do not pretend to have made many, but it is a real pleasure to know that I have lost none.

We have sent for Dr. Aikin's Annals, which we never heard of till now.

Believe me to be sincerely yours,

RICHD. LOVELL EDGEWORTH."

" My dear Mrs. Barbauld,

Your kind, warm, friendly letter, has set my heart at ease, upon a subject which has long been very painful to me. I feared, and I could not bear to think, that I had lost that place in your esteem and affection, with which I knew that you once honoured me. I could not bear the idea, that you suspected me of being so weak, so vain, so senseless, as to have my brain turned by a little fashionable flattery, and to have so changed my character, as not to feel the difference between *your friendship*, and the common-place compliments of *Lady This* and *That and T'other*. Your letter has dissipated all the very painful fancies, and real fears that have been growing and preying upon me these two years. Thank you—' *on the knees of my heart* ' I thank you. And be assured that your condescension and goodness, in begging my pardon, when I ought to have begged, and did a hundred times in my secret soul beg yours, is not thrown away upon me.

So we will now go on where we left off, too long ago. I will write whenever I have anything to say that I wish to say to you, whether it be worth your hearing or not; and if you do not answer me, I will only *regret*, I promise you I will never be angry, nor will I ever more fret myself, with the notion, that you are angry with me. God bless Mrs. Baillie, for breaking the ice between us.

You have no idea how long, how terribly long, it is, before books of any substantial merit, reach this remote ultimate Edgeworthstown. Such trash as ' Glenarvon' and such mischief as ' Bertram' comes too fast, poisoning all the wind. We have book societies in the country, and do order books of merit and reputation ; but it is a tedious time before the Dublin booksellers get them, as they dare not write for them on their own account. I shall immediately bespeak Dr. Aikin's Annals for our society. We shall anxiously expect Miss Aikin's Reign of Elizabeth. Have you seen a book of Dr. Millar's, on the Philosophy of History ? The introductory chapter is well done, but I fear there is a *vice de construction* in the plan of the book. The witty, bitterly witty, Plunket told him, that with such a plan, he should not have published the book, *till the day of Judgment.* His plan, you know, is to shew, that all history forms a moral drama. Now, till the drama is finished,

Q

how can he come to the moral, and without omniscience, how can he see the connexion of the parts and the whole.

I have lately seen a poem, which reminded me of the *spirit* of your ' 1811.' I do not mean to say in the versification, for that is unharmonious, and often defective, but I admire in it the noble spirit of patriotism and virtue. His *classical taste* and *Anti-Byron* principles. The poem I mean is *'Greece'* by Mr. Haygarth. I know nothing of him, but I think if he cultivates his interests, he may either become a fine historian, or a fine tragedian. This praise implies a great range of mind, but I do not say he is—I say he may become—all this, —and I should very much wish to know whether you think the same.

On the contrary, I do not think that the author of ' Bertram,'* though he has written a successful tragedy, will ever write a good tragedy—feeling run mad!—

As to ' Glenarvon,' it surely can *do* no mischief, it is such nonsense. I stuck fast

---

* The Rev. R. C. Maturin.

in the blood and love in the second volume, and in that condition, fell fast asleep, and never would have opened my eyes on the third volume, but that my father begged me to read the death of the Princess of Madagascar, which seems, with all that relates to the Princess, to be written by a pen, much superior to Lady Caroline Lamb's.—Who wrote it? Is it known?

We have just got a little book called 'Display,' a tale for young people, which we like much. It is written by the daughter of a physician, a Miss Jane Taylor, who keeps a school near Dublin. I am not acquainted with her. The *good* people in this book, are more to my taste, than those in Cœlebs, because they are not so meddling. I only wish they had not objected to young people going to balls. Before I could finish my sentence, in praise of all the good sense and excellent writing of this tale, a circle of young and old ladies were open-mouthed with the question,—but why object to balls? I hope you like the Antiquary. And I hope you have no doubt of its having been written by Walter Scott.

We have just received two numbers of a new 'Journal of the Arts and Sciences,' edited at the Royal Institution of Great Britain. Like it much. Glad to see Sir Humphrey Davy's lamp lighting him back to the paths of Science, from the bootless excursion he took into the land of fashion. Better be the first, than the last of a class. Better be the first man of science, than the last man of fashion.—Especially as he can be the one, and cannot be the other.

In the first number of this Journal, there is a paper, by Dr. Park, on the laws of sensation, which my father admires very much.

I think the *nerves* will give physicians and philosophers, enough to do for the next century. The *humorers* have had their day.

Here is a gentleman in our neighbourhood, who one year imagines himself to be without bones, and another year without muscles, and one year is a Harry-long-legs, and another a man; and all the time, eats and drinks heartily, and wears a coat like other men, and is not considered as *more* than nervous.

I will now finish, lest you should repent having let loose my pen upon you. My father has been better lately; but his health is far from strong. I say as little as I can upon this subject, it is too near my heart. Mrs. Edgeworth is in as blooming, happy, and useful health as when you knew her at Clifton.

I wish, my dear Mrs. Barbauld, I could transport you into this large cheerful family, where every body,—from little Pakenham at four years old, to the old housekeeper, 'eldest of forms,' would do every-thing in their power to make you feel quite at home. You should never see any washing-day* but *one.*

Your friend, Lord Longford, has just written us word that he is going to be married, and from his own and the impartial account of his dear sister—(commonly called the Duchess of Wellington), the lady he has chosen will not only permanently please himself but satisfy the anxious

---

* A playful poem of Mrs. B's given in the Appendix.

wishes of his host of family friends. She is Lady Georgina Lygon, tenth daughter of Lord Beauchamp. He says she will not permit him to be an 'absentee', so we shall now have him again settled at Pakenham Hall, within ten miles of us. Now, my dear Mrs. Barbauld, could not you summon up resolution enough to be sea sick for six hours, say ten at the utmost, to make us happy, and I hope yourself, for as many months ! I have two brothers now at Cheltenham, Lovell and Sneyd, both known to you, both coming over to Ireland, Mrs. Sneyd E. also—could you not come with them ? Anna (Mrs. Beddoes) also coming in the spring.

Think of what has been said ! and do not tremble at the thoughts of my pestering you often with such long letters, for I assure you it is not my habit, but in the warmth of heart kindled by your warm affectionate letter all this poured out.

Your affectionate, obliged
and grateful friend,
MARIA EDGEWORTH."

To Miss Edgeworth.

" Dear Madam,

I am penetrated with your kind-
ness, your frank forgiveness and the valued
favour of your long letter. For your kind
invitation too I sincerely thank you, nor
could anything be more attractive than the
society to which you invite me, not to
mention the attraction of a country, interesting, and to me new, but indeed I am now
too old to travel, or shall I rather say, I
expect to take a journey longer than that,
and to a country more unknown. Short
excursions indeed I do not disclaim, and
am now just returned from a visit to Mr.
W. Smith * of Parndon, whose family I believe you know. He is now one of the
oldest members of the House of Commons
that we have, and· has always been very
steady to his principles, but he was then as
busy as an old Roman in getting in his
harvest. Patty Smith, the eldest and most
accomplished, is in very indifferent health,
I am sorry to say. My brother is delighted

---

* Mr. William Smith M.P. for Norwich.

that you are pleased with Mr. Haygarth's
Poem, for the author is the son of a very
intimate friend of his, a Physician, who
died lately at Bath, or rather near it, and
left his son in circumstances to indulge all
his elegant tastes without being confined
to any profession; he is now again upon
his travels. I think his Poem elegant and
beautiful, but you will excuse my differing
from you, if I say that I should rather
reverse the character you give of his
genius, and the author of Bertram; for
Haygarth seems to me to have already
attained nearly the acme of his, grace,
elegance, classic taste; but in Bertram,
along with much that is dark, wild, and
repulsive, equally to taste and moral sense,
I think I see sparks of a high genius and
more capabilities of improvement—*Au reste*,
pray do not reproach us with sending you
'Bertram,' you sent it us. I have not
seen Dr. Millar's publication, but I can
hardly allow to Plunket that in a good
Drama you must wait for the conclusion
before you can form *any* opinion of the

catastrophe of the piece. We judge by the bearings. Who doubts long before the conclusion of the piece, that Desdemona's innocence will become apparent, and Othello die in agonies of remorse, but in the great Drama of the Universe, the difficulty is to see the *bearings*. Turner in his History of the Anglo-Saxons, a work of great research, has attempted something of this kind, but I think without much success. 'Display' we sent for on your recommendation, and are much pleased with a good deal of it, but we are entirely of your opinion with regard to balls, and indeed there is a great deal in her system that I should object to, particularly the doctrine, which I think a very pernicious one, that all, the innocent and good as well as the bad, must undergo a mysterious change before they are in a safe state. Emily was very good for aught that I could see before her conversion. I trembled, as I drew near the close, lest Elizabeth should have a fine fortune left her by somebody, and was much pleased with the author's good sense in handing

her to her post behind the counter. By the
way, are you not mistaken in the Author?
We take it to be the production of *Jane
Taylor* of *Ongar*, who has written several
pieces, both verse and prose, for children.
I am just entering on 'Mrs. Marcet's
Conversations on Political Economy,' a
new subject for a Lady's pen. You are I
believe personally acquainted with Mr.
Roscoe, I send you the enclosed sonnet
to show how well he bears the bitter depri-
vation, to a man of letters and of taste, of
his noble collection of books and paintings.
Among the curiosities of literature let me
ask if you have seen the Rimini of Leigh
Hunt? An author, who, in exaggeration
of all the slovenliness of the new school,
has thought proper to come into public with
his neckcloth untied and his stockings about
his heels.

My dear Miss Edgeworth, though I shall
never see, I enjoy your account of Edgeworthstown. I do not conceive a more
agreeable abode, and beg to be remembered
to every individual of it. I rejoice much in

the approaching happiness of Lord Longford and the more because, if he is what he
was, I believe him fully qualified to appreciate and enjoy domestic pleasures. If he
is so good as to remember me pay my compliments. My nephew Arthur Aikin and
his friends have been in the bustle of
canvassing for some weeks past. He is
soliciting for the situation of *Secretary to the
Society of Arts,** vacant by the death of Mr.
Taylor, and with a very fair prospect of
success. He has sixteen hundred members
to canvass and being naturally rather taci-
turn and very modest, we have been amused
to think how he would acquit himself, but
he says he improves in assurance every day.
In point of literary and scientific merit, none
of the candidates can pretend to stand a
comparison with him. My dear Miss
Edgeworth, if I did as I ought to do, I
should write this bad scrawl, full of blunders, over again, but then I should lose my

---

* He held this office for twenty years, and that of
Chemical Lecturer of Guy's Hospital for almost as long
a time afterwards. A short notice of him by his sister
Lucy Aikin, will be found in the Appendix.

frank, so you must excuse it, and believe me ever your obliged, affectionate,

A. L. BARBAULD."

September 17th, 1817.

To Mr. Rogers.

" Dear Sir,

My Brother and Sister as well as myself are very truly sensible of the favour of your invitation, nor are we insensible of the entertainment* which Monday evening will afford, notwithstanding which we must with sincere thanks decline so tempting an offer. With regard to Lucy, whose youth and spirits would best have borne the fatigue of such a day, or rather night, and might have communicated enjoyment as well as received it, she is at Liverpool. Suffer me to add with regard to myself, I feel sensibly touched with the *kindness* which prompted you to think of me on this occasion, distant as I am from you, and little able as I feel myself to return by *mine* the pleasure I

---

* The fireworks and illuminations for the Peace with France.

always receive from *your* company. I have another instance of attention from you which has for some time demanded my thanks, a most elegant little poem,* which as its parent did not choose to own it, was left to disclose its parentage by its merits. You scorn to take advantage of the fame you are in possession of, and choose to surprise the admiration you might command. I hope this is an earnest of more, and as I see you can with readiness take any style and manner you please, I shall be upon the watch for you whenever I see anything particularly elegant.

Adieu dear Sir, and believe me no one is more desirous of your esteem or sensible to your friendship than your obliged and faithful,

A. L. BARBAULD.

Excuse blunders, I write with children about me."

She received about this time a visit from one who seems to form a link with the

---

* Jacqueline.

succeeding age, Dr. Channing, who alludes to it in a letter to Miss Aikin after Mrs. Barbauld's death.

"Boston, Feb. 27th, 1827.

I thank you, as thousands have done for your tribute to the memory of Mrs. Barbauld, and I am peculiarly indebted to you for the present of her works.

I can remember Mrs. B's poetry from early life, and I owe her more than delight. Some of her pieces we may suppose she will recollect for ever with pleasure, for they have lifted many minds to that pure world in which she has found rest. Much of the prose volume was new to me, and I felt that she had not received the praise due to her in this species of composition. I was struck with the felicity of the style, and the freshness and animation and frequently the originality of her thoughts.

I remember my short interview with her with much pleasure. Perhaps I never saw a person of her age who had preserved so much of youth—on whom time had laid so

gentle a hand. Her countenance had
nothing of the rigidness and hard lines of
advanced life, but responded to the mind
like a young woman's. I carry it with me
as one of the treasures of memory."

Mr. Crabb Robinson also in one of his
last visits to her, remarks, as well as Dr.
Channing, upon her personal appearance.
"I called on the Colliers, and then went
to Mrs. Barbauld's. She was in good
spirits, but she is now the confirmed old
lady. Independently of her fine understanding, and literary reputation, she
would be interesting. Her white locks,
fair and unwrinkled skin, brilliant starched
linen, and rich silk gown, make her a fit
object for a painter. Her conversation is
lively, her remarks judicious, and always
pertinent." (Mr. Robinson's Diary.)

A letter to Miss Edgeworth, and the
fragment of verse which follows it, are
almost her last writings.

" My dear Miss Edgeworth,

I was very glad to see your hand writing again, and to hear that your pen was again in employment, that pen which has already given us so much pleasure, and from which, I hope, the world may expect pleasure and improvement for many years to come.

The Enigma* you do me the honour to ask for, will accompany this, but I have first to find it, for though I have looked a good deal, I have not yet been able to lay my hands on it. I beg to make proviso, that if I should want myself to insert it in any publication, I may be at liberty to do it. Though, truly, that is not very likely, for well do I feel, one faculty after another withdrawing, and the shades of evening closing fast around me, and be it so. What does life offer at past eighty, (at which venerable age, I arrived one day last June,) and I believe you will allow, that there is not much of new, of animating, of inviting, to be met with after that age. For my own

---

* In the Appendix.

part, I only find that many things I knew
I have forgotten, many things I *thought* I
knew, I find I knew nothing about ; some
things, I know, I have found not worth
knowing, and some things I would give—
Oh ! what would one not give to know, are
beyond the reach of human ken. Well, I
believe this is what may be called prosing,
and you can make much better use of your
time than to read it. I saw yesterday two
boys, modern Greeks, in the costume of
their country, introduced by Mr. Bowring,
who has the charge of them.—du Grec, ah
ma sœur du Grec, ils parlent du Grec ! I
have been reading one or two American
novels lately. They are very well, but I do
not wish them to write novels yet. Let
them explore and describe their new
country. Let them record the actions of
their Washington, the purest character perhaps, that history has to boast of ; let them
enjoy their free, their unexpensive government, number their rising towns, and boast
that persecution does not set her bloody foot
in any corner of their extensive territories.

R 2

Then let them kindle into poetry, but not
yet, not till the more delicate shades and
nicer delineations of life are familiar to
them, let them descend to *novels*. But
tempted, by writing to you, I am running
on, till my eyes are tired, and perhaps you
too. Compliments to Mrs. Edgeworth and
all your family. If I find the riddle, I will
send it you, mean while, I am, with the
truest esteem and friendship, dear Miss
Edgeworth, your affectionate friend,

A. L. BARBAULD.

Stoke Newington,
   Oct. 25th, 1823.''

> Fall, fall! poor leaf, that on the naked bough,
> Sole lingering spectacle of sad decay,
> Sits shivering at the blasts of dark November;
> Thy fellows strew the ground, not one is left
> To grace thy naked side; late who could count
> Their number multitudinous and thick,
> Veiling the noon-day blaze, behind their shade
> The birds half-hid disported; clustering fruit
> Behind their ample shade lay glowing ripe;
> No bird salutes thee now; nor the green sap
> Mounts in thy veins, thy spring is gone, thy summer;
> Even the crimson tints,

Thy grave but rich autumnal livery,
That pleased the eye of contemplation—
Some filament perhaps, some tendril stronger
Than all the rest, resists the whistling blast.
Fall, fall, poor leaf,
Thy solitary single self shews more
The nakedness of winter,
Why wait and fall, and strew the ground like them?

The following is taken from Miss Aikin's Memoir.

"An asthmatic complaint which was slowly undermining her excellent constitution, more and more indisposed her for any exertion either of mind or body; but the arrival of a visitor had always the power to rouse her from a state of languor. Her powers of conversation continued to the last though her memory of recent circumstances became somewhat impaired. Her disposition, (of which sensibility was not in earlier life the leading feature,) now mellowed into softness, pleasingly exhibited. 'those tender tints that only time can give.' Her manners—never tainted by pride—which with the baser but congenial affection of envy was a total stranger to her bosom,

were now remarkable for their extreme
humility; she spoke of every one not merely
with the candour and forbearance which
she had long practised, but with interest
and kindness, with an indulgence which
sometimes appeared but too comprehensive;
she seemed reluctant to allow or believe
that any of her fellow creatures had a failing,
while she gave them credit gratuitously for
many virtues. This state of mind, which
with her native acuteness it must have cost
her some struggles to attain, had at least
the advantage of causing her easily to admit
of such substitutes as occurred for those con-
temporary and truly congenial friendships,
which in the course of nature were now
fast failing her. She lost her early and
affectionate friend Mrs. Kenrick in 1819.
In December 1822 her brother sunk under
a long decline which had served as a pain-
full preparation to the final parting. A few
months later she lost in the excellent Mrs.
John Taylor of Norwich, perhaps the most
intimate and highly valued of all her distant
friends.

A gentle and scarcely perceptible decline was now sloping the passage to the tomb. She felt and hailed it as a release from languor and infirmity, a passport to another and higher state of being. Her friends however flattered themselves that they might continue to enjoy her a little longer, and she had consented to remove to the house of her adopted son, that his affectionate attention and those of his family might be the solace of every remaining hour. But Providence had ordained it otherwise. She quitted indeed her own house, but whilst on a visit to the neighbouring one of her sister-in-law Mrs. Aikin, the constant and beloved friend of nearly her whole life, her bodily powers gave way almost suddenly, and after lingering a few days she expired without a struggle, on the 9th of March 1825, in the eighty second year of her age.

To claim for this distinguished woman the praise of purity and elevation of mind, may well seem superfluous. Her education and connections, the course of her life, the whole tenour of her writings, bear testimony to this part of her character. It is a higher, or at least a rarer commendation to add that no one ever better loved ' a sister's praise,' even that of such sisters as might have been peculiarly regarded in the light of rivals. She was acquainted with almost all the principal female writers of her time, and there was not one whom she failed to mention in terms of admiration, esteem, or affection. To humbler aspirants, who often applied to her for advice or assistance, she was invariably courteous, and often serviceable. The sight of youth and beauty was peculiarly gratifying to her fancy and feelings, and children and young persons were large sharers in her benevolence ; she loved their society, and would often invite them to spend weeks and months in her house, where she spared no pains to amuse and instruct them, and she seldom failed to recall herself to their recollection, by affectionate and playful letters, or welcome presents.

In the conjugal relation, her conduct

was guided by the highest principles of
love and duty. As a sister, the uninterrupted flow of her affection, manifested by
numberless tokens of love—not alone to her
brother, but to every member of his family,
will ever be recalled by them, with emotions
of tenderness, respect, and gratitude. She
passed through a long life, without having
dropped, it is believed, a single friendship,
and without having drawn upon herself
a single enmity which could be called
personal."

Though in the preceding pages, Mrs.
Barbauld's literary character has been
chiefly dwelt upon, it would be an imperfect
view of it, which did not include some notice
of her deep interest in the cause of civil
and religious liberty.

Living as she did, through times in which
the profession of liberal opinions was in the
highest degree unpopular, not to say dan-
gerous, she never hesitated to employ all
her gifts of eloquence and reasoning, to
endeavour to bring about a better state of
things, and as a dissenter especially, to free

those who shared her opinions, from the social disabilities, which after the lapse of many years were happily removed.

On the defeat of a Bill brought before Parliament in 1790, for the repeal of the Corporation and Test Acts, she wrote a powerful and eloquent pamphlet, which though anonymous, was soon recognised as hers. The following letters addressed to her, among many others, at that time, from Mr. Rogers, and Dr. Moore the author of Zeluco, and father of General Sir John Moore, show the appreciation of the liberal party of her efforts on this occasion.

" Newington Green, March 29th, 1790. Dear Madam,

I have read over and over again the address to the opposers of the Repeal, and cannot sufficiently thank you for having first suggested it to my notice ; though its spirit and elegance are now indeed the subject of universal admiration and curiosity. Its author may elude our search for a little while, but cannot long remain undiscovered.

Its fine irony, its elevation and sublimity
of sentiment, will soon blaze out the secret,
though 'wrapt in tenfold night.' And
whoever has read the essays of a lady whose
superior genius every one has the discern-
ment to see and admire except yourself, is
already, I think, in the possession of a clue
that cannot fail to direct his inquiries.

I remain with great respect,

Dear Madam, your obliged

Friend and Servant,

Saml. Rogers.

I beg my best Compts.
to Mr. Barbauld."

" To the Revd. Rochemont Barbauld,
Clifford Street,
29 Nov. 1790.

Dear Sir,

When I had the pleasure of seeing
Mrs. Barbauld and you at your house at
Hampstead, I had not read her address to
the opposers of the repeal of the Test Acts,
but I had heard a report of her intending
to answer Mr. Burke's famous pamphlets,

s

—and I confess I heard this with some degree of concern, for notwithstanding the high opinion I had formed of her talents, I could not help being a little uneasy at the thoughts of her entering the lists with so formidable an antagonist—but I have just finished the perusal of her address, and all my fears are vanished. I hardly know anything in the English language superior in delicacy of irony, and strength of reasoning, to that truly eloquent performance. And in my opinion she could not employ her time more to her own honour and the public benefit, than by publishing her sentiments on Mr. Burke's works.

I beg you will offer my respectful thanks to Mrs. Barbauld for the pleasure I received from her pamphlet, which I sincerely think the most elegant and most judicious production that has issued from the press for a very long time.

I am dear Sir, with much esteem,
Your obedient humble servant.
T. MOORE."

In a letter to a friend announcing the death of her, who had been to him as a mother, Mr. Charles Rochemont Aikin concludes with the following passage.

"I will fill this page with a few lines which will interest you, as being I believe, the very last which my venerable aunt committed to paper when she felt the hand of death approaching her. It is a few unfinished sentences, but to me deeply interesting."

"Who are you?
Do you not know me, have you not expected me?
Whither do you carry me?
Come with me and you shall know.
The way is dark.
It is well trodden.
Yes, in the forward track.
Come along!
Oh, shall I see there my beloved ones, will they welcome me, will they know me, oh, tell me, tell me, thou canst tell me?
Yes, but thou must come first.
Stop a little, keep thy hand off till thou hast told me!
I never wait.
Oh shall I see the warm sun again in my cold grave?

Nothing is there that can feel the sun.
Oh where then ?
Come, I say."

Mrs. Barbauld was buried in the family vault of Dr. Aikin in Stoke Newington Church-yard.

Shortly after her death Mr. C. R. Aikin was requested by the congregation of Newington Green Chapel, where she had attended as long as her strength allowed, to place some memorial of her upon their walls.

A marble tablet was therefore erected by him with the following inscription written by her nephew Arthur Aikin.

EPITAPH.

———◆———

IN MEMORY OF

ANNA LETITIA BARBAULD,

DAUGHTER OF JOHN AIKIN, D.D.

AND WIFE OF

THE REV. ROCHEMONT BARBAULD,

FORMERLY THE RESPECTED MINISTER OF THIS CONGREGATION.

SHE WAS BORN AT KIBWORTH IN LEICESTERSHIRE, 20TH JUNE, 1743,
AND DIED AT STOKE NEWINGTON, 9TH MARCH, 1825.

ENDOWED BY THE GIVER OF ALL GOOD
WITH WIT, GENIUS, POETIC TALENT, AND A VIGOROUS UNDERSTANDING
SHE EMPLOYED THESE HIGH GIFTS
IN PROMOTING THE CAUSE OF HUMANITY, PEACE, AND JUSTICE,
OF CIVIL AND RELIGIOUS LIBERTY,
OF PURE, ARDENT, AND AFFECTIONATE DEVOTION.

LET THE YOUNG, NURTURED BY HER WRITINGS IN THE PURE SPIRIT
OF CHRISTIAN MORALITY;
LET THOSE OF MATURER YEARS, CAPABLE OF APPRETIATING
THE ACUTENESS, THE BRILLIANT FANCY, AND SOUND REASONING
OF HER LITERARY COMPOSITIONS ;
LET THE SURVIVING FEW WHO SHARED HER DELIGHTFUL
AND INSTRUCTIVE CONVERSATION,
BEAR WITNESS
THAT THIS MONUMENT RECORDS
NO EXAGGERATED PRAISE.

APPENDIX.

APPENDIX.

From the Rev. Dr. Doddridge to Miss Jennings,
(afterwards Mrs. Aikin.)

Dr. Mad.^{m.}

    I owe Dear Miss Jenny and her good
Mamma my earliest Thanks for all the Pleasure I
had in the Company of both at Harborough, and
must confess that when I left it I hardly expected
so much as I found in conversing with Miss Cotton
at Maidwell. It seems to me that I am going into
a kind of Solitude when I am leaving you, but it
prov'd otherwise on Fryday and Saturday. Besides
the Satisfaction I always find in the Conversation of
so valuable a Friend as Lady Russel, the Lady I
mention'd before gave me a great Deal. I know
you hear this with a charitable Pleasure and flatter
your self with a secret Hope that she is making a
Conquest on a fond Heart from which you might
apprehend some farther Trouble, of that Mad.^m you
will judge when I tell you, that the most delightful

part of her Conversation was that which turn'd upon
her Father and Mother of whom she gave me the
following Account which I humbly recommend to
your serious Perusal.

Mr. Cotton was turn'd of 30 when he fell in
Love w^h the Lady who is now his Wife. She was
then like your self a gay beautiful Creature just in
the Bloom of fifteen, in whom that truly wise and
good Man discern'd those early Marks of Piety
Genius Politeness good Humour and Discretion
which I am more and more admiring in you, and
which engage him to prefer her to those whose Age
might have seem'd more suitable to his own. He
pursued his Addresses with all possible Application
and exerted in her Service all the Tenderness with
which so charming a Creature could inspire him and
all the politeness which he had learnt from a most
liberal Education and several years Travels thro'
Italy and France in the Company of some Persons
of great Distinction which renders him thus late in
the Evening of Life incomparably more agreeable
than the generality of Mankind in its Morning or
Meridian. Miss Biddy (for that was her name)
heard him with all the Indifference in the World for
two years together and often declares that tho' she
treated him civily as a Gentleman and a Friend and
the rather out of Regard to her Mamma who had a
great Regard and Affection for him yet she never

entertain'd any Thoughts of Love to him till within three Weeks of their Marriage. At last she gave him her Heart with her hand in the 17th year of her Age and yᵉ 33ᵈ of his. And it is now almost half a Century that she has been rejoicing in it as the kindest Providence of her Life. They have been still the Joy of their Friends and each other and are concluding an honourable and a delightful Life together as gracefully and as amiably as any Couple I ever knew; and I verily believe that she is as dear to him now tho' she is rather older than he was in the first Months of their Marriage.

I might make a variety of pertinent and useful Reflections on this most entertaining and edyfying Story but I shall content my self with mentioning two and refer the rest to your private Meditations.

It is possible (you see) for a Man of a very agreeable and valuable Character in Life and for a Minister too, deliberately to chuse and passionately to love a Lady considerably younger than himself, even an Infant of 15 (and how much more one who will be 16 in October) And he may continue for Life fond and proud of that Choice.

And than secondly and lastly (which is to me much more surprizing than the former) that a Lady of that tender and impressible age may hear a Courtship (not the dullest or most despicable in the World) for two years together without any Sentiment of Love or Thoughts of Marriage and yet afterwards receive it with an intire Consent and that peculiar Pleasure which I suppose Nothing upon Earth can give but the Surrender of the Heart to a worthy Man who has deserv'd it by a long Course of Service and Sufferings.

You must pardon me Madam if after all this I conclude with my hearty wishes that if we live to the year 1770 a Daughter every Way as agreeable and valuable as Miss Cotton may he telling the same Story (as far as the inferiority of my Character will admit) of the lovely Trifler who is now smiling at so extravagant a Thought

and her most affectionate Friend

and obliged humble Servant.

P. DODDRIDGE.

Northampton, May 29th, 1730.

Your Aunt Norris went away this morning. Pray give my best services to your Dear Mamma, not forgetting my other Friends at Harborough. I long and yet I fear to see you.

I hope to be wth you in a few Days, but will keep your Brother here so long as I stay myself.

BISHOP BONNER'S GHOST,

By Mrs. Hannah More—written 1789.

In the gardens of the palace at Fulham is a dark recess, at the end of this stands a chair which once belonged to Bishop Bonner. A certain Bishop (Porteus) more than 200 years after the death of the aforesaid Bonner, one morning undertook to cut with his own hand a narrow walk through this thicket. He had no sooner begun, than lo! suddenly up started from the chair the Ghost of Bishop Bonner, who in a tone of just and bitter indignation uttered the following verses.

> Reformer hold ! ah spare my shade,
> Respect the hallowed dead ;
> Vain prayer, I see the op'ning glade,
> See utter darkness fled.
>
> Just so your innovating hand,
> Let in the moral light ;
> So chased from this bewilder'd land,
> Fled intellectual night.

T

Where now that holy gloom which hid,
Fair truth from vulgar ken;
Where now that wisdom which forbid,
To think that monks were men.

The tangled mazes of the schools,
Which spread so thick before;
Which knaves entwin'd to puzzle fools,
Shall catch mankind no more.

Those charming intricacies, where?
Those venerable lies?
Those legends, once the Church's care,
Those sweet perplexities?

Ah! fatal age, whose sons combined,
Of credit to exhaust us;
Ah! fatal age, which gave mankind
A Luther and a Faustus.

Had only Jack and Martin lived,
Our power had slowly fled;
Our influence longer had survived,
Had laymen never read.

For knowledge flew, like magic spell,
By Typographic art;
Oh shame! a peasant now can tell,
If priests the truth impart.

Ye councils, pilgrimages, creeds!
Synods, decrees, and rules!
Ye warrants of unholy deeds,
Indulgences, and bulls.

Where are ye now? and where alas!
The pardons we dispense?
And penances the sponge of sins;
And Peter's holy pence?

Where now the beads which used to swell,
Lean virtue's spare amount?
Here only faith and goodness fill,
A heretic's account.

But soft—what gracious form appears?
Is this a convents' life,
Atrocious sight! by all my fears,
A prelate with a wife!

Ah! sainted Mary not for this
Our pious labours joined,
The witcheries of domestic bliss
Had shook e'en Gardiner's mind.

Hence all the sinful, human ties,
Which mar the cloister's plan;
Hence all the weak fond charities,
Which make man feel for man.

But tortured memory vainly speaks,
The projects we design'd;
While this apostate bishop seeks,
The freedom of mankind.

Oh, born in everything to shake,
The systems plann'd by me !
So heterodox that he would make,
Both soul and body free.

Nor clime nor colour stays his hand,
With charity deprav'd,
He would from Thames to Gambia's strand,
Have all be free and sav'd.

And what shall change his wayward heart,
His wilful spirit turn ?
For those his labours can't convert,
His weakness will not burn.

A GOOD OLD PAPIST.

"THE APOLOGY OF THE BISHOPS,"
IN ANSWER TO "BONNER'S GHOST."

By Mrs. Barbauld.

Right Revd. Brother and so forth
The Bishops send you greeting,
They honour much the zeal and worth
In you so highly meeting.

But your abuse of us, good Sir
Is very little founded !
We blush that you should make a stir
With notions so ill grounded.

'Tis not to us should be addrest
Your ghostly exhortation,
If heresy still lifts her crest
The fault is in the nation.

The State, in spite of all our pains,
Has left us in the lurch,
The spirit of the times restrains
The spirit of the Church.

To this day down from famed Sacheverel
Our zeal has never cooled,
We mean to Truth and Freedom ever ill,
But we are over ruled.

Still damning Creeds framed long ago,
Help us to vent our spite ;
And penal laws our teeth to shew
Although we cannot bite.

Our spleen against reforming cries
Is now as ever shewn ;
Though we can't blind the nation's eyes
We still can shut our own.

T 2

210

Well warned from what abroad befalls,
We keep all tight at home ;
Nor brush one cobweb from St. Paul's,
Lest it should shake the dome.

Once in an age a Louth may chance
To wield the pastoral staff,
And Fortune for a whim advance
A————————or——————*

Yet do not thou by fears misled
To rash conclusions jump,
So little leaven scarce appears,
And leaveneth *not* the lump.

What though the arm of flesh be dead
And lost the power it gives,
The spirit quickeneth, it is said,
And sure the spirit lives.

The Birmingham Apostle then,†
And Essex Street Apostate,‡
Debarred from paper and from pen
Should both lament their lost state.

Church maxims do not greatly vary,
Take it upon my honour,
Place on the throne another Mary,
We'll find her soon a Bonner.

---

* A———— or———— Hoadly or Landaff ?
† Dr. Priestley.   ‡ The Revd. Theophilus Lindsey.

WASHING-DAY.

. . . . and their voice,
Turning again towards childish treble, pipes
And whistles in its sound.——

The Muses are turned gossips ; they have lost
The buskined step, and clear high-sounding phrase,
Language of gods. Come then, domestic Muse,
In slipshod measure loosely prattling on
Of farm or orchard, pleasant curds and cream,
Or drowning flies, or shoe lost in the mire
By little whimpering boy, with rueful face ;
Come, Muse, and sing the dreaded Washing-Day.
Ye who beneath the yoke of wedlock bend,
With bowed soul, full well ye ken the day
Which week, smooth sliding after week brings on
Too soon ;—for to that day nor peace belongs
Nor comfort ;—ere the first gray streak of dawn,
The red-armed washers come and chase repose.
Nor pleasant smile, nor quaint device of mirth,

E'er visited that day : the very cat,
From the wet kitchen scared and reeking hearth,
Visits the parlour,—an unwonted guest.
The silent breakfast-meal is soon dispatched ;
Uninterrupted, save by anxious looks
Cast at the lowering sky, if sky should lower.
From that last evil, O preserve us heavens !
For should the skies pour down, adieu to all
Remains of quiet : then expect to hear
Of sad disasters,—dirt and gravel stains
Hard to efface, and loaded lines at once
Snapped short,—and linen-horse by dog thrown down,
And all the petty miseries of life.
Saints have been calm while stretched upon the rack,
And Guatimozin smiled on burning coals ;
But never yet did housewife notable
Greet with a smile a rainy washing-day.
—But grant the welkin fair, require not thou
Who call'st thyself perchance the master there,
Or study swept, or nicely dusted coat,
Or usual 'tendance ;—ask not, indiscreet,
Thy stockings mended, though the yawning rents
Gape wide as Erebus ; nor hope to find
Some snug recess impervious ; shouldst thou try
The 'customed garden walks, thine eye shall rue
The budding fragrance of thy tender shrubs,
Myrtle or rose, all crushed beneath the weight
Of coarse checked apron,—with impatient hand
Twitched off when showers impend : or crossing lines
Shall mar thy musing, as the wet cold sheet

Flaps in thy face abrupt. Woe to the friend
Whose evil stars have urged him forth to claim
On such a day the hospitable rites !
Looks, blank at best, and stinted courtesy,
Shall he receive. Vainly he feeds his hopes
With dinner of roast chicken, savoury pie,
Or tart or pudding :—pudding he nor tart
That day shall eat; nor, though the husband try,
Mending what can't be helped, to kindle mirth
From cheer deficient, shall his consort's brow
Clear up propitious :—the unlucky guest
In silence dines, and early slinks away.
I well remember, when a child, the awe
This day struck into me ; for then the maids,
I scarce knew why, looked cross, and drove me from them:
Nor soft caress could I obtain, nor hope
Usual indulgencies, jelly or creams,
Relic of costly suppers, and set by
For me their petted one ; or buttered toast,
When butter was forbid ; or thrilling tale
Of ghost, or witch, or murder—so I went
And sheltered me beside the parlour fire :
There my dear grandmother, eldest of forms,
Tended the little ones, and watched from harm,
Anxiously fond, though oft her spectacles
With elfin cunning hid, and oft the pins
Drawn from her ravelled stocking, might have soured
One less indulgent.—
At intervals my mother's voice was heard,
Urging dispatch : briskly the work went on,

All hands employed to wash, to rinse, to wring,
To fold, and starch, and clap, and iron, and plait.
Then would I sit me down, and ponder much
Why washings were.   Sometimes through hollow bowl
Of pipe amused we blew, and sent aloft
The floating bubbles; little dreaming then
To see, Mongolfier, thy silken ball
Ride buoyant through the clouds—so near approach
The sports of children and the toils of men.
Earth, air, and sky, and ocean, hath its bubbles,
And verse is one of them—this most of all.

L I F E .

Animula, vagula, blandula.

Life ! I know not what thou art,
But know that thou and I must part ;
And when, or how, or where we met,
I own to me's a secret yet.
But this I know, when thou art fled,
Where'er they lay these limbs, this head,
No clod so valueless shall be,
As all that then remains of me.
O whither, whither, dost thou fly,
Where bend unseen thy trackless course,
   And in this strange divorce,
Ah tell where I must seek this compound I ?
To the vast ocean of empyreal flame,
    From whence thy essence came,
    Dost thou thy flight pursue, when freed
    From matter's base encumbering weed ?
     Or dost thou, hid from sight,
     Wait, like some spell-bound knight,

Through blank oblivious years th' appointed hour,
To break thy trance and reassume thy power?
Yet canst thou without thought or feeling be?
O say what art thou, when no more thou'rt thee?

Life! we've been long together,
Through pleasant and through cloudy weather;
  'Tis hard to part when friends are dear;
  Perhaps 't will cost a sigh, a tear;
  Then steal away, give little warning,
    Choose thine own time;
Say not Good night, but in some brighter clime
    Bid me Good morning.

ENIGMA.

We are spirits all in white
On a field as black as night,
There we dance and sport and play
Changing every changing day;
Yet with us is wisdom found
As we move in mystic round.
Mortal, wouldst thou know the grains
That Ceres heaps on Libya's plains,
Or leaves that yellow Autumn strews,
Or the stars that Herschel views,
Or find how many drops would drain
The wide-scooped bosom of the main,
Or measure central depths below,—
Ask of us, and thou shalt know.
With fairy feet we compass round
The pyramid's capacious bound
Or step by step ambitious climb
The cloud-capt mountain's height sublime.
Riches though we do not use
'Tis ours to gain, and ours to lose.
From Araby the Blest we came
In every land our tongue's the same;
And if our number you require

U

Go count the bright Aonian quire.
Wouldst thou cast a spell to find
The track of light, the speed of wind,
Or when the snail with creeping pace
Shall the swelling globe embrace ;
Mortal, ours the powerful spell ;—
Ask of us, for we can tell.

(FIGURES ON A SLATE.)

ARTHUR AIKIN, was born at Warrington in Lancashire, May 19, 1773, and died in London in 1854.

He was the eldest son of John Aikin M.D. long and honorably distinguished in the world of letters.

In Arthur the family vocation declared itself from infancy. He could read well before he had completed his second year. In his seventh, his father entered him at the excellent Free School of his native town. The start thus gained was never lost. He derived from his father, together with an ardent love of literature, ancient and moden, a zeal for several of those branches of science which he cultivated with the most success in after life; for Zoology, to the study of which his father had been incited by his intimate correspondence with Mr. Pennant; for English Botany, and for Chemistry, a visit at the age of twelve in the house of Dr.

Priestley, then pursuing at Birmingham, his brilliant course of chemical discovery, confirmed him in his predilection for this science.

The destination of the grave and studious boy was early fixed for the Christian Ministry. After some years passed under the tuition of Mr. and Mrs. Barbauld he became a student of the New College at Hackney, and a favorite pupil in their respective lines of the learned Gilbert Wakefield, and of Dr. Priestley, who delighted him by claiming his assistance in the arrangement of his *new* laboratory.

Mr. Aikin was for nearly two years one of the Ministers of a highly respectable congregation at Shrewsbury.

At the end of this time, from motives which did him nothing but honour, he relinquished his profession, but not his connection with that part of the country; he made several tours in Wales, of one of which he published an interesting and instructive account, and he was the first to investigate and describe the geology of Shropshire.

Henceforth his home was in London; and for many years in the house of his beloved brother the late Mr. Charles Aikin, in conjunction with whom he published in 1797 the Chemical Dictionary. In this work the separate articles are not assigned to their respective authors, so intimate was the concert between the Brothers, so equally shared

the labour and the ability ! Through a long career
he preserved without the smallest deviation, " the
even tenor of his way." A total absence of ambition ; a natural shyness which shrunk from all
display ; a taciturnity often painful and mortifying
to his friends, withheld him from ever taking in
mixed society, or in general estimation the place
which his eminent abilities, his scientific skill, and
the extraordinary variety, extent, and accuracy of
his knowledge, justly entitled him; on the other
hand he never engaged in a controversy and never
made an enemy. His wants were few, his manners
simple, kind and courteous, his affections tender and
constant ; his temper was imperturbable ; his charity
unfailing, his disinterestedness exemplary, his morals
spotless.

AGAINST INCONSISTENCY

IN OUR

EXPECTATIONS.

———

1773.

AGAINST INCONSISTENCY IN OUR EXPECTATIONS.

———◆———

" WHAT is more reasonable, than that they who
" take pains for any thing, should get most in
" that particular for which they take pains?
" They have taken pains for power, you for right
" principles; they for riches, you for a proper use
" of the appearances of things: see whether they
" have the advantage of you in that for which you
" have taken pains, and which they neglect: If
" they are in power, and you not, why will not
" you speak the truth to yourself, that you do
" nothing for the sake of power, but that they do
" every thing? No, but since I take care to have
" right principles, it is more reasonable that I
" should have power. Yes, in respect to what
" you take care about, your principles. But give
" up to others the things in which they have
" taken more care than you. Else it is just as

"if, because you have right principles, you should
"think it fit that when you shoot an arrow, you
"should hit the mark better than an archer, or
" that you should forge better than a smith."
CARTER'S EPICTETUS.

As most of the unhappiness in the world arises
rather from disappointed desires, than from positive
evil, it is of the utmost consequence to attain just
notions of the laws and order of the universe, that
we may not vex ourselves with fruitless wishes, or
give way to groundless and unreasonable discontent.
The laws of natural philosophy, indeed, are tolerably
understood and attended to; and though we may
suffer inconveniences, we are seldom disappointed in
consequence of them. No man expects to preserve
orange-trees in the open air through an English
winter; or when he has planted an acorn, to see it
become a large oak in a few months. The mind of
man naturally yields to necessity; and our wishes
soon subside when we see the impossibility of their
being gratified. Now, upon an accurate inspection,
we shall find, in the moral government of the world,
and the order of the intellectual system, laws as determinate, fixed, and invariable, as any in Newton's
Principia. The progress of vegetation is not more

certain then the growth of habit; nor is the power
of attraction more clearly proved than the force of
affection or the influence of example. The man
therefore who has well studied the operations of
nature in mind as well as matter, will acquire a
certain moderation and equity in his claims upon
Providence. He never will be disappointed either
in himself or others. He will act with precision;
and expect that effect, and that alone, from his efforts,
which they are naturally adapted to produce. For
want of this, men of merit and integrity often censure
the dispositions of Providence for suffering characters
they despise to run away with advantages which,
they yet know, are purchased by such means as a
high and noble spirit could never submit to. If you
refuse to pay the price, why expect the purchase?
We should consider this world as a great mart of
commerce, where fortune exposes to our view various
commodities, riches, ease, tranquillity, fame, integrity, knowledge. Every thing is marked at a settled
price. Our time, our labour, our ingenuity, is so
much ready money which we are to lay out to the
best advantage. Examine, compare, choose, reject;
but stand to your own judgement; and do not, like
children, when you have purchased one thing, repine
that you do not possess another which you did not
purchase. Such is the force of well-regulated industry, that a steady and vigorous exertion of our

faculties, directed to one end, will generally insure
success. Would you, for instance, be rich? Do
you think that single point worth the sacrificing
every thing else to? You may then be rich.
Thousands have become so from the lowest begin-
nings by toil, and patient diligence, and attention
to the minutest articles of expense and profit. But
you must give up the pleasures of leisure, of a
vacant mind, of a free unsuspicious temper. If you
preserve your integrity, it must be a coarse-spun
and vulgar honesty. Those high and lofty notions
of morals which you brought with you from the
schools, must be considerably lowered, and mixed
with the baser alloy of a jealous and worldly-mind-
ed prudence. You must learn to do hard, if not
unjust things; and for the nice embarrassments of
a delicate and ingenuous spirit, it is necessary for
you to get rid of them as fast as possible. You must
shut your heart against the Muses, and be content
to feed your understanding with plain, household
truths. In short, you must not attempt to enlarge
your ideas, or polish your taste, or refine your sentiments; but must keep on in one beaten track,
without turning aside either to the right hand or to
the left. "But I cannot submit to drudgery like
this—I feel a spirit above it." 'Tis well: be above
it then; only do not repine that you are not rich.

Is knowledge the pearl of price? That too may

be purchased—by steady application, and long solitary hours of study and reflection. Bestow these, and you shall be wise. "But (says the man of letters) what a hardship is it that many an illiterate fellow who cannot construe the motto of the arms on his coach, shall raise a fortune and make a figure, while I have little more than the common conveniences of life." *Et tibi magna satis !*—Was it in order to raise a fortune that you consumed the sprightly hours of youth in study and retirement? Was it to be rich that you grew pale over the midnight lamp, and distilled the sweetness from the Greek and Roman spring? You have then mistaken your path, and ill employed your industry. "What reward have I then for all my labours?" What reward! A large comprehensive soul, well purged from vulgar fears and perturbations, and prejudices; able to comprehend and interpret the works of man—of God. A rich flourishing, cultivated mind, pregnant with inexhaustible stores of entertainment and reflection. A perpetual spring of fresh ideas; and the conscious dignity of superior intelligence. Good heaven! and what reward can you ask besides?

"But is it not some reproach upon the economy of Providence that such a one, who is a mean dirty fellow, should have amassed wealth enough to buy half a nation?" Not in the least. He made him-

w

self a mean dirty fellow for that very end. He has paid his health, his conscience, his liberty for it; and will you envy him his bargain? Will you hang your head and blush in his presence because he outshines you in equipage and show? Lift up your brow with a noble confidence, and say to yourself, I have not these things, it is true; but it is because I have not sought, because I have not desired them; it is because I possess something better. I have chosen my lot. I am content and satisfied.

Your are a modest man—You love quiet and independence, and have a delicacy and reserve in your temper which renders it impossible for you to elbow your way in the world, and be the herald of your own merits. Be content then with a modest retirement, with the esteem of your intimate friends, with the praises of a blameless heart, and a delicate ingenuous spirit; but resign the splendid distinctions of the world to those who can better scramble for them.

The man whose tender sensibility of conscience and strict regard to the rules of morality makes him scrupulous and fearful of offending, is often heard to complain of the disadvantages he lies under in every path of honour and profit. "Could I but get over some nice points, and conform to the practice and opinion of those about me, I might stand as fair a chance as others for dignities and preferment."

And why can you not? What hinders you from discarding this troublesome scrupulosity of yours which stands so grievously in your way? If it be a small thing to enjoy a healthful mind, sound at the very core, that does not shrink from the keenest inspection; inward freedom from remorse and perturbation; unsullied whiteness and simplicity of manners; a genuine integrity

"Pure in the last recesses of the mind;"

if you think these advantages an inadequate recompense for what you resign, dismiss your scruples this instant, and be a slave-merchant, a parasite, or—what you please.

"If these be motives weak, break off betimes;"

and as you have not spirit to assert the dignity of virtue, be wise enough not to forego the emoluments of vice.

I much admire the spirit of the ancient philosophers, in that they never attempted, as our moralists often do, to lower the tone of philosophy, and make it consistent with all the indulgences of indolence and sensuality. They never thought of having the bulk of mankind for their disciples; but kept themselves as distinct as possible from a worldly life. They plainly told men what sacrifices were required, and what advantages they were which might be expected.

> "Si virtus hoc una potest dare, fortis omissis
> Hoc age deliciis........"

If you would be a philosopher these are the terms.
You must do thus and thus: there is no other way.
If not, go and be one of the vulgar.

There is no one quality gives so much dignity to
a character as consistency of conduct. Even if a
man's pursuits be wrong and unjustifiable, yet if
they are prosecuted with steadiness and vigour, we
cannot withhold our admiration. The most characteristic mark of a great mind is to choose some
one important object, and pursue it through
life. It was this made Cæsar a great man. His
object was ambition; he pursued it steadily, and
was always ready to sacrifice to it every interfering
passion or inclination.

There is a pretty passage in one of Lucian's dialogues, where Jupiter complains to Cupid that
though he has had so many intrigues, he was never
sincerely beloved. In order to be loved, says Cupid,
you must lay aside your ægis and your thunder-
bolts, and you must curl and perfume your hair, and
place a garland on your head, and walk with a soft
step, and assume a winning obsequious deportment.
But, replied Jupiter, I am not willing to resign so
much of my dignity. Then, returns Cupid, leave off
desiring to be loved—He wanted to be Jupiter and
Adonis at the same time.

It must be confessed, that men of genius are of all others most inclined to make these unreasonable claims. As their relish for enjoyment is strong, their views large and comprehensive, and they feel themselves lifted above the common bulk of mankind, they are apt to slight that natural reward of praise and admiration which is ever largely paid to distinguished abilities; and to expect to be called forth to public notice and favour: without considering that their talents are commonly very unfit for active life; that their eccentricity and turn for speculation disqualifies them for the business of the world, which is best carried on by men of moderate genius; and that society is not obliged to reward any one who is not useful to it. The poets have been a very unreasonable race, and have often complained loudly of the neglect of genius and the ingratitude of the age. The tender and pensive Cowley, and the elegant Shenstone, had their minds tinctured by this discontent; and even the sublime melancholy of Young was too much owing to the stings of disappointed ambition.

The moderation we have been endeavouring to inculcate will likewise prevent much mortification and disgust in our commerce with mankind. As we ought not to wish in ourselves, so neither should we expect in our friends contrary qualifications. Young and sanguine, when we enter the world, and

feel our affections drawn forth by any particular
excellence in a character, we immediately give it
credit for all others; and are beyond measure dis-
gusted when we come to discover, as we soon must
discover, the defects in the other side of the balance.
But nature is much more frugal than to heap together all manner of shining qualities in one glaring
mass. Like a judicious painter she endeavours to
preserve a certain unity of style and colouring in her
pieces. Models of absolute perfection are only to be
met with in romance; where exquisite beauty, and
brilliant wit, and profound judgement, and imma-
culate virtue, are all blended together to adorn some
favourite character. As an anatomist knows that
the racer cannot have the strength and muscles of
the draught horse; and that winged men, griffins,
and mermaids must be mere creatures of the imagination; so the philosopher is sensible that there
are combinations of moral qualities which never can
take place but in idea. There is a different air and
complexion in characters as well as in faces, though
perhaps each equally beautiful; and the excellencies
of one cannot be transferred to the other. Thus if
one man possesses a stoical apathy of soul, acts independent of the opinion of the world, and fulfills
every duty with mathematical exactness, you must
not expect that man to be greatly influenced by the
weakness of pity, or the partialities of friendship :

you must not be offended that he does not fly to meet you after a short absence; or require from him the convivial spirit and honest effusions of a warm, open, susceptible heart. If another is remarkable for a lively active zeal, inflexible integrity, a strong indignation against vice, and freedom in reproving it, he will probably have some little bluntness in his address not altogether suitable to polished life ; he will want the winning arts of conversation; he will disgust by a kind of haughtiness and negligence in his manner, and often hurt the delicacy of his acquaintance with harsh and disagreeable truths.

We usually say—that man is a genius, *but* he has some whims and oddities—such a one has a very general knowledge, *but* he is superficial; &c. Now in all such cases we should speak more rationally did we substitute *therefore* for *but*. He is a genius, *therefore* he is whimsical; and the like.

It is the fault of the present age, owing to the freer commerce that different ranks and professions now enjoy with each other, that characters are not marked with sufficient strength: the several classes run too much into one another. We have fewer pedants, it is true, but we have fewer striking originals. Every one is expected to have such a tincture of general knowledge as is incompatible with going deep into any science; and such a conformity to fashionable manners as checks the free workings of the ruling passion, and gives an insipid sameness to the face of society, under the idea of polish and regularity.

There is a cast of manners peculiar and becoming to each age, sex, and profession; one, therefore, should not throw out illiberal and common-place censures against another. Each is perfect in its kind. A woman as a woman : a tradesman as a tradesman. We are often hurt by the brutality and sluggish conceptions of the vulgar; not considering that some there must be to be hewers of wood and drawers of water, and that cultivated genius, or even any great refinement and delicacy in their moral feelings, would be a real misfortune to them.

Let us than study the philosophy of the human mind. The man who is master of this science, will know what to expect from every one. From this man, wise advice; from that cordial sympathy; from another, casual entertainment. The passions and inclinations of others are his tools which he can use with as much precision as he would the mechanical powers; and he can as readily make allowance for the workings of vanity, or the bias of self-interest in his friends, as for the power of friction, or the irregularities of the needle.

FINIS.